To Damian,

The truth will
you free.

Freddy Da

THE
TRUTH MIRAGE

THE
TRUTH MIRAGE

AN INTRODUCTION TO WORLDVIEW
FOR BIBLICAL CHRISTIANS

by

FREDDY DAVIS

LEADERSHIP
Books

THE TRUTH MIRAGE
© 2019 by Freddy Davis

ISBN: 978-0-9916453-4-3 (hardcover)

Publisher:
Vision Group, Limited, The
www.LeadershipBooks.net

Published September 2019
Printed and distributed by Ingram Press

Graphic Design:
KAnneDesigns

TABLE OF CONTENTS

Table of Contents

Continued

Introduction

Over the last several years, I have spent a lot of time and effort studying worldview, writing books about it, giving presentations, and preparing training materials. I am so passionate about it because I believe that an understanding of worldview provides Christians with powerful resources that help them live out the Christian faith in our modern pluralistic world. It gives us the knowledge we need to grasp the truth and its implications for our own faith in their fullness, the ability to understand other faiths, and tools to enable our witness for Christ effectively.

But that is not all. An understanding of worldview gives us a couple of other important things, as well. For one, it helps us grasp a more in-depth sense of what we, and others, believe. Beyond that, it gives us a way to understand *why* what we believe is the truth and *why* other beliefs are not the truth.

In previous generations in America, grappling with the "why" element of our faith was not so critical. In an era when pretty much everyone in the culture believes the same thing (or, at least, acts as though they do), a person's worldview beliefs are not really challenged. Up until, perhaps, the 1960s, America was still very homogeneous–religiously. That is, at the very least, the massive majority did believe in God (or, at least, acted as though they did). And most of them actually believed in the God of the Bible. In an environment like that, people were not really asking why the Christian faith was the truth. They just assumed it to be so and went on with their lives–even if they were not faithfully living out a biblical lifestyle.

Well, things have radically changed. America is no longer the religiously homogeneous, Judeo-Christian nation it used to be. We have become a very pluralistic society with all of the major

> *"Well, things have radically changed. America is no longer the religiously homogeneous, Judeo-Christian nation it used to be."*

cultural institutions now dominated by an entirely different worldview.

Of course there have always been those who didn't believe in God. However, in the late 1800s when Darwin put forth his Theory of Evolution, it gave this atheistic faction the cover it needed to begin pushing for dominance. From that time forward, people with a naturalistic worldview began deliberately and intentionally inserting themselves into the nation's various cultural institutions. And slowly but surely, they began to gain dominance.

I believe the tipping point came in the 1960s and 70s, and it has only become stronger since that time. In fact, now the naturalistic worldview literally dominates every facet of the culture–family, entertainment, education, media, government, and business. Sadly, it has even made huge strides in many churches and Christian denominations.

There is only one way for Christians to gain back influence in the culture, and that is for believers to do exactly what the Naturalists did. We must deliberately and intentionally inject ourselves, with our faith, back into the institutions of the culture and win in the arena of ideas. True change only comes with a change of hearts and minds.

But to turn things around, it is not enough simply to convince people that our beliefs are superior–which they are, by the way. Intellectual superiority alone will not win the day. People who have turned away from God did not simply decide that

Naturalism is intellectually superior. Rather, they literally converted to a belief system that does not include God. The turn-around must involve people being converted back to a Biblical belief in God.

Understanding how to fight this worldview war requires something of Christians that was not necessary in times past. When everyone basically shared the same worldview, all we needed to share with people was how to know Christ. In the past, for the most part, the only people who needed to grasp worldview concepts were missionaries who went to places where other worldviews dominated. But that is simply not the case anymore.

Now, a majority of people in our own nation do not share our worldview. Because of that, a witness for Christ must very often be preceded by a worldview explanation. This is necessary because the very concepts of the Christian faith do not make sense to those who hold a different worldview. Those who hold other worldview beliefs actually think their beliefs are true and that ours are false—and they live daily life based on this "Truth Mirage."

And that is the purpose of this book—to help everyday believers stand strong in their faith as they live life in our increasingly pluralistic culture.

In times past, a study of worldview was primarily an academic pursuit. It used to be that the books written about it were primarily done by academics for academics. Today, that will not do. Every believer needs to understand this topic and be able to use it in their faith life and witness. It is my hope and prayer that this book will contribute to the strengthening of your faith life and witness. On top of that, I pray that God will use you more and more to accomplish his work in the world.

Consider this ...

Radical Islamists have a history of employing the most brutal and barbaric tactics. They have particularly become known for beheading people.

- In one case, 75 Syrian soldiers at a military base were captured by militant Islamists and were beheaded. The militants displayed the soldier's heads and bodies along the streets.
- In another case, the Islamists beheaded about 100 foreign fighters—who were actually fighting alongside them—because they believed these soldiers were deserting.
- Another case saw 10 Egyptian men beheaded because the radical Islamists believed they were spies.
- Then there was the case where the Islamists beheaded 21 Coptic Egyptians in Tripoli, Libya—because they were Christians.
- There was another case where the militants shot and beheaded 28 Ethiopian Christians in Libya—also simply because they were Christians.

Since this book was published, the incidents of murder and mayhem have not diminished. If you want to know the latest atrocities, all you need to do is read the headlines in this week's media. These have continued because committing these acts is an integral part of the very belief structure of the people who are doing it. They believe that when they kill infidels, they are doing the will of God. Militant Islamists consider anyone who disagrees with their particular religious beliefs to be worthy of death. This includes Christians, journalists, Muslims who are not Muslim enough for their tastes, people they consider spies, enemy combatants and, really, just about anyone who is against them for any reason·

What do you think it is about the beliefs of Radical Islamists that makes them think that slaughtering people this way is okay?

Chapter 1

Worldview Differences: The Basis for All Cultural Conflicts
DOES EVERY PATH LEAD TO THE TOP OF MT. FUJI?

You have, no doubt, heard about many different kinds of wars as you have listened to the news: world wars, regional wars, gang wars, the war on women, racial wars, proxy wars, religious wars, culture wars, gender wars, conventional wars, asymmetrical wars, wars of resistance, independence wars, class wars, tribal wars, civil wars, sectarian wars, guerrilla wars, the cold war, nuclear war … and we could probably go on and on with this list.

As we look at these different kinds of wars, most of them don't really seem to have any connection with one another. Some relate to nationalistic issues, others to ethnic and cultural issues, religious issues, stylistic issues, weapons issues, and so on. But in spite of the seeming disconnect between the different categories, they all have one element in common. That element exists at the most fundamental level possible. At the root of every kind of war is a faith system that deems it okay to fight the war.

> *"At the root of every kind of war is a faith system that deems it okay to fight the war."*

For some reading this, the idea of a faith system being at the root of every kind of war may seem a bit of a stretch. But is it a stretch, really? Let's look at some examples and identify the faith underlying them.

World wars, regional wars, tribal wars, the cold war—In these cases, national leaders in various countries **BELIEVED**

that they either had the right to take over other countries, or defend themselves from those who felt they did.

Gang wars, proxy wars, wars of resistance, independence wars, civil wars—In these cases, groups of people **BELIEVE** they have the right to exert their will over people who live in "their" territory, or defend themselves from those who were trying to take over.

The war on women, gender wars, race wars, culture wars, class wars—Here we have situations where people **BELIEVE** they have a right to put down others who are different from themselves, or defend themselves from people who are attacking them for that reason.

Religious wars, sectarian wars—These are cases where people **BELIEVE** their religious faith condones the use of violence to overcome other religious **BELIEFS**.

Conventional wars, asymmetrical wars, nuclear war—In these cases we are dealing with people's **BELIEFS** about what can be considered legitimate means for fighting wars.

> *"[Everything] we think and do is built on a faith foundation?" It means that there is no scientifically verifiable way to prove the most basic elements of reality."*

When we get down to the bottom line, the thing all of them have in common is an appeal to a set of beliefs. Of course, it is not just the matters related to wars that have their basis in a faith system. The truth is, EVERYTHING we think and do is built on a faith foundation. If we want to understand the reason people (ourselves included) think what they think and do what they do, we must understand their faith system. That is to say, we must understand their worldview and their beliefs.

The Pervasiveness of Faith Systems

So, exactly what are we talking about when we say "everything we think and do is built on a faith foundation?" It means that there is no scientifically verifiable way to prove the most basic elements of reality. While at first this approach to looking at conflict may seem a bit academic, it is far from it. In fact, it is the most practical approach we can possibly take. While these things may be studied in academia, every conflict is <u>expressed</u> in real life and affect the life experience of real people—yourself included. So, let's look a little deeper and see how this plays out. What, exactly, do we mean when we say "everything is built upon a faith system?"

There are those who believe that it is possible to empirically or scientifically prove that what they believe about reality is true. This would particularly involve those who believe in a naturalistic worldview. Naturalists believe that science can be used to explain every part of life. Beyond that, they believe this to be so self-evident, that anyone who believes differently must believe in magic.

However, no understanding of reality actually has science as its exclusive foundation. No one can prove, using empirical means, that what they believe is true. Let's look, for a moment, at what kind of proof would actually be required to give scientific verification for a worldview belief.

The first requirement would be a demonstration—using experimental science—that the material which makes up the physical universe had a natural origin. This would be necessary because this material forms the basis of their belief

---

"[What] we believe must ultimately have its foundation in a set of assumptions – assumptions that cannot be demonstrated using experimental science. They are based purely on faith."

---

that everything which exists is material—in a natural universe—and can be explained based on the natural laws of the universe. But, if the things we think we know about the properties and operation of the natural universe are not known by science, then we must believe them by faith. We do know that the material universe exists—don't we? We seem to have identified laws of nature that govern it: yet there is no scientific knowledge concerning where the material, or even the laws themselves, come from. So, when it comes to this topic, what we believe must ultimately have its foundation in a set of assumptions—assumptions that cannot be demonstrated using experimental science. They are based purely on faith.

A second necessary proof for a naturalistic worldview would be an empirical demonstration of how life came into existence. Obviously, life exists, or does it? Again, there are those who believe that what we perceive as life is actually an illusion. But even for those of us who believe it actually exists, we have no way to demonstrate, using experimental science, where life came from. What we believe about life's origin must be believed by faith.

A third element of reality that cannot be empirically demonstrated is the origin of the vast variety of life forms which exist on our planet. Of course, there are those who have come up with elaborate theories to account for a naturalistic basis for all life forms. But in order to back their theories, they have to first assert "beliefs" about the structure of reality which they cannot demonstrate using experimental science. There is no empirical science that can definitively account for the variety of life that exists on the earth. What people believe about this topic must be believed by faith.

Finally, there is no empirical accounting for the origin of consciousness. Interestingly, there are even people who claim that there is no such thing as consciousness. Of course, they have to justify their belief using a conscious process. There are others who believe that consciousness is illusory in other ways: for instance, determinists would say that consciousness is an illusion based purely on the operation of chemical and biological processes in the brain. The point is, no matter what anyone believes about the origin of consciousness, it must be believed by faith. There is no experimental science that is able to show where consciousness came from.

The Limits of Empiricism

There is a way reality is actually structured. The only problem is, there is no way to come to an understanding of this actual structure using only empirical means. Those who will only accept scientific proof as the basis for describing reality are just out of luck. There is no such proof. While there is a natural part of reality that people can get at using experimental science, there are parts that simply cannot be accessed that way. This is true no matter what one believes about how reality is structured. Logic, deduction, and human experience, which are not necessarily accessible using empirical methods, are also essential to the process.

This is certainly not meant to belittle science in any way. Since we are physical beings and live in an objectively real physical universe that operates by natural laws, there are parts of reality which are accessible and measurable by empirical methods. But even that does not get at the entirety of reality. There are parts of it which must be addressed using different means.

We looked, above, at some of the serious problems of a purely empiricist worldview.

- How does one explain the origin of the matter and energy that exists in the material universe?
- How does one explain the origin of life?
- What natural processes empirically explain the variety of life forms that exist on earth?
- What is the origin of consciousness?
- How does one explain human self-consciousness?

None of these questions can be answered using purely empirical methods. All of them require exploration using methods that go beyond empirical proof. They all require that we begin using a set of faith presuppositions; and from there, build an explanatory system to support our beliefs. In addition to empirical methodologies, we must also throw logic, deduction, and human experience into the mix.

There is another important point that we must understand. The fact that we must ultimately approach our beliefs about reality using faith assumptions does not necessarily mean that our beliefs are based on "blind" faith. Reality does exist in some real form, and there is some actual way of explaining what that form looks like. It is just that the evidence we use to reach our conclusion must rely on more than just scientific methodologies. We must come to the place where we acknowledge that the use of logic, deduction, and human experience are also essential components. When we attempt to describe actual reality, it must make sense using ALL of the lines of evidence—empirical science, logic, deduction, and human experience. The fact that our starting place is a point of faith does not mean it is untrue. When all of the forms of evidence line up, truth is assured. It is just that no belief system can be demonstrated using only empirical methodologies.

The Two Kinds of Faith Systems

After acknowledging that faith is the ultimate foundation for everything everyone believes, we must then drill down a little deeper to grasp the nature of the faith systems within which we operate. There are actually two different kinds of faith systems which work in tandem with one another, only on different levels. The first is made up of worldview systems, and the second of belief systems: we will get into these much more deeply as we move forward, but it will be helpful to at least understand this distinction early on.

"A worldview system is a set of beliefs that defines the way we understand reality."

Worldview Systems

A worldview system is a set of beliefs that defines the way we understand reality. These beliefs are so fundamental that everyone, without exception, finds it unimaginable that other people would not accept them. After all, if we perceive something to be real, how could anyone possibly not agree with it. They would have to be living in a fantasy world to not see things the way we see them, right? In fact, for most people, these beliefs are so foundational that they are held at an unconscious level. If you were to go around and ask random people to tell you their most basic beliefs—what they believe at a worldview level—they would likely not be able to give you a satisfactory answer. They would probably start telling you, instead, about their "belief system."

Belief Systems

The second faith system category is a belief system. This represents the various religions, cults, and philosophies that exist in the world. These are the beliefs that people hold at a conscious level, and can generally be expressed by a doctrinal statement. All belief systems are built on the foundation of a particular worldview system, and will have the same foundational beliefs as its worldview parent.

> *"[A] belief system ... represents ... the beliefs that people hold at a conscious level, and can generally be expressed by a doctrinal statement."*

The Basis of All Conflict

So, with that basic introduction, we circle back to the origin of the various wars people fight. We can now see that when people try to find the reason for conflict, they generally look at the "belief system" level. They do that because belief system differences are most obvious at the conscious level. But in truth, belief systems provide only shallow, surface-level explanations. The true

> *"But in truth, belief systems provide only shallow, surface-level explanations. The true basis for most conflict is generally found at the worldview level, not the belief system level."*

basis for most conflict is generally found at the worldview level, not the belief system level.

Now of course, this is not exclusively true. There are battles between people who fight over matters at the belief system level. Typically, these are people who are either looking to exert personal power, or have exaggerated the importance of relatively unimportant beliefs. At the deepest level, however, the most intensity is generated at the worldview level. This is the place where a person's very identity is invested. This is the place where an individual's understanding of reality is stored. This is the place where a person's ultimate passion will make its final stand.

> *"[The] worldview level ... is the place where a person's very identity is invested. This is the place where an individual's understanding of reality is stored. This is the place where a person's ultimate passion will make its final stand."*

Discussion Questions

1. What kinds of human activities are not based on a faith system?
2. What is the difference between a worldview system and a belief system?
3. What kinds of proofs are valid for legitimizing a faith system?
4. What can and cannot be proven by empiricism?
5. What kinds of conflict are based on belief systems, and what kinds are based on worldview systems?

Consider this ...

I've had the opportunity to engage in many conversations with activist Atheists. Among these, only an occasional, stray person actually understands their Atheism. Honestly, most are totally clueless about their atheistic faith. In the course of these interactions, there are four things that keep emerging in the discussions.

First, I have noticed that these activist Atheists are militant because Atheism is their religion. As individuals who are committed to their faith, most simply cannot, and will not, tolerate conflicting beliefs.

A second thing that typically emerges is that they don't understand the implications of their own beliefs. Atheism cannot live up to its own requirements; which makes the faith of its adherents completely irrational.

A third thing that generally emerges is that these militants don't understand the Christian faith. In spite of that, they have no hesitation about attacking my Christianity using bogus arguments.

My final observation is that most activist Atheists have a powerful, even if unjustified, confidence that their beliefs are true. This reflects the fact that their Atheism is based on a set of beliefs that define reality for them: they cannot imagine reality existing any other way.

What benefits will a Christian gain by understanding worldview?

Chapter II

Why Understanding Worldviews is Important
How do you know that what you believe is real?

As I have shared worldview training with Christians over the years, many of them had a difficult time not only understanding the concept of worldviews, but even identifying why Christians need to know anything about it. In fact, I have seen people get downright hostile and even attempt to silence me because of their belief that "if we will just share the gospel, we don't need anything else."

Now, I will be the first to affirm that no one can come to Christ until they accept the gospel—and the gospel message has never changed. That said, if we share the gospel—but the people with whom we share it do not understand the underlying concepts of what we are sharing—can we actually say we have shared it?

Suppose you go to someone who only speaks Chinese and share very clearly and completely the gospel message—in English. Is it reasonable to claim that you have actually shared the gospel with that person if they don't understand a word you are saying? Of course not! If they do not understand your words, all you have shared with them is noise.

Let's take this scenario one step further: suppose you share the

> *"Is it reasonable to claim that you have actually shared the gospel with that person if they don't understand a word you are saying?"*

gospel in English with another person who speaks English, but their entire life experience causes them to misinterpret the meaning of the concepts you share. What you end up with is exactly the same problem. For instance, suppose every time you used the word "God," their understanding of the word caused them to associate your words with Allah. And every time you used the word salvation, their understanding related to the "Five Pillars" of the Islamic faith? And what if every time you talked about Jesus, their understanding was that He was the prophet who preceded Mohammed? While the words you said might have been understandable based on the language, the person you shared with did not understand the meaning you were trying to convey. It is not enough to only speak their physical language, you must also speak their conceptual language. The topic of worldview deals with people's conceptual language.

At this point, I can read your thoughts. You are thinking something like, "This sounds so-o-o academic." Or, "This is wa-a-ay beyond my ability to understand."

"It is not enough to only speak their physical language, you must also speak their conceptual language. The topic of worldview deals with people's conceptual language."

Okay, just stop that kind of thinking right now.

While worldview can be studied in an academic environment (as can construction, computers, hair styling, welding, law, theology and virtually every other subject), worldview is actually very practical, and, when presented in the right way, it is not that difficult to grasp. It is so practical, in fact, that there is not a single part of your life that is not an expression of your worldview beliefs; including everything you think, everything you say, and everything you do.

My question to you is, "If worldview beliefs are, indeed, so foundational, wouldn't it be wiser to make a little effort to understand them, rather than ignoring them and pretending they are too difficult to understand?" I think the answer should be rather obvious. So, let's begin by doing a short examination of the things that a knowledge of worldview can do for us.

Worldview is the foundation of all our thoughts and actions.

It is hard to overestimate the power of a person's worldview beliefs.

The fact is, not all beliefs are held with equal value. Some are very lightly held, and people are quite willing to change them without much pressure. Others are held at an emotionally deeper level and can only be changed after a certain amount of deep thought, or even struggle.

But worldview beliefs go even deeper than that. In fact, worldview beliefs exist at such

"[Worldview beliefs] seem so obvious they are not even questioned: they are simply assumed to be true. [They] serve as the basis of all thoughts and actions. ... a person's worldview establishes the ultimate core of their very concept of self."

a deep level that most people are not even consciously aware of them. They seem so obvious they are not even questioned: they are simply assumed to be true. These beliefs serve as the basis of all thoughts and actions. As such, a person's worldview establishes the ultimate core of their very concept of self.

The fact that worldview beliefs are so powerful is a clue as to why it is important for Christians to understand worldview concepts. When we think about our own spiritual growth, and about sharing a witness for Christ, we are automatically drilling down to the worldview level. The more we are able to understand this level of our beliefs, the better we will be able to engage the various parts of our faith.

Understanding worldview helps us truly understand our own faith.

Understanding worldview involves exploring the most basic foundation of a faith system. This certainly applies to the non-Christian beliefs we encounter as we interact with people out in the world, but it applies to our own beliefs, as well. If we want to know the most fundamental elements of our Christian faith, we must look to the particular beliefs that make up its worldview foundation. When we truly grasp this foundation, we will be in a position to comprehend our Christian faith in a way that leads to true understanding.

When it comes to any faith system, there is a set of essential elements that form its core. One cannot tamper with these elements and remain a part of that faith system. However, there are other beliefs that, while they may hold importance, do not rise to the level of being essential. You can believe or not believe non-essentials, and they don't take you out of the domain of the belief system itself. Part of truly understanding our own faith

"An understanding of worldview gives us a basis [to] distinguish between the essentials and non-essentials."

involves being able to distinguish between the essentials and non-essentials. An understanding of worldview gives us a basis for doing this.

Understanding worldview helps us understand the beliefs of other people.

As Christians, one of the most important things God has tasked us with is sharing our faith. This is not such a difficult thing if the people with whom we are interacting already understand the basic concepts—*i.e.,* the worldview that underlies our Christian faith. However, there are an increasing number of people who don't share our basic understanding. Their faith foundation—their worldview—is something entirely different from ours. If that is the case, becomes necessary for us to build a conceptual bridge from our Christian worldview to whatever their worldview beliefs may be—so they can understand the gospel message when we share it. It is this understanding of these worldviews that gives us the ability to grasp other faith systems, in order to build that bridge.

Understanding worldview helps us have confidence that our faith is the truth.

One last important outcome of understanding worldview relates to the confidence it gives us as we interact with people who hold other belief systems. In our modern culture, there are more and more people who not only hold to competing faith systems, but who are militant in their advocacy for their beliefs. There is no shortage of people attempting to push Christianity and Christians out of the public square. This is a serious problem for those who do not know how to stand up against those bullies. An understanding of worldview helps us deal with this problem.

> "The fact is, there is an actual structure to reality, and our Christian faith represents that structure."

The fact is, there is an actual structure to reality, and our Christian faith represents that structure. The key to standing confidently in our faith is to not only understand "what" we believe, but also "why" what we believe is the truth. Our Christian faith does, in fact, stand up to scrutiny, while other belief systems do not. When we understand why this is so, our confidence in standing up against opposition will soar.

Understanding worldview is very practical.

The topic of worldview does not fit into the traditional way Christians have thought about living out or sharing their faith. Because of that, there tends to be a certain amount of ambivalence, and sometimes even hostility, to injecting it into the mix of our discipleship training. But that is a very short-sighted point of view. Our culture has certainly changed. While that does not change the gospel message, it does change how our faith interacts with the beliefs of those who are not Christians. There are now massive numbers of people who simply do not understand even the most basic concepts of the Christian faith. So even if we clearly share the gospel message, they will not understand what we are talking about. There are others who self-identify as Christians, yet are so confused by the many belief systems now inhabiting the public square, that they are silent about their faith. Some even begin to doubt it.

An understanding of worldview deals with all of these problems. It provides confidence concerning the truthfulness of our Christian faith, and is a means for bridging the conceptual gap between our faith and other faith systems. Rather than shying away from the topic of worldview, Christians ought to be jumping in with both feet to gain the most profound understanding possible.

Discussion Questions

1. What is it about a worldview that causes it to be the foundation of all our thoughts and actions?
2. How does an understanding of worldview help us more completely understand our own faith?
3. What does an understanding of worldview give us that helps us better grasp the beliefs of other faiths?
4. Why does an understanding of worldview help Christians have confidence in their faith?
5. What is it about an understanding of worldview that makes it a practical topic of study?

Consider this ...

When I first took the opportunity to learn about other beliefs, I studied them by reading books about different religions, such as Islam, Mormonism, Jehovah's Witnesses, and so on. At that time, it was an interesting study, but I was left a bit dissatisfied. The main reason was that after reading about two or three of them, the information began getting jumbled up in my head. There were just too many details to keep up with.

Later I became dissatisfied for a different reason. My study assumed that the Christian faith was right and the other beliefs were wrong, but there was no real way to compare them for truth.

In some ways, that was not too big a problem back then because Christianity was still the dominant belief system in the country. There just were not a lot of people militantly attacking my faith. That is simply not the way things are now. Modern day America has become very pluralistic, and it is not at all uncommon to interact with people who come from other belief systems. If we truly want to understand them, we must have a way of not only getting at what they believe, but also evaluating for truth.

So, I began studying other ways of dealing with the various belief systems. But even with that I was left feeling dissatisfied. Although some approaches were better than others, there was still a problem when trying to compare them with one another and evaluating for truth; and without the ability to do that, it is just one person's opinion against another.

Is there a way to get at the truth as it relates to religious belief?

Chapter III

Approaches to Understanding Faith Systems
IS THERE A RIGHT WAY TO STUDY RELIGION?

A s we look at the concept of faith systems, it is very easy
to fall into the trap of treating them as mere academic
subjects. Certainly, we can study them academically in
order to learn as much as possible. But, the true nature of a faith
system cannot be fully grasped by only learning its doctrine.
Ultimately, the beliefs must be played out in real life: it is the
effect on individual life and society that gets us down to the true
implications of a faith. The truth is, we live every part of our lives
based on how we perceive reality, and the reality we perceive is
based on a faith system.

As we try to understand faith systems, we need to recognize
that we cannot truly understand them based on a single facet.
It is much like a diamond, with different facets that must all be
understood. In particular, we need to look at where faith systems
come from, and then at the various categories of faith systems
that exist. It is by understanding these aspects that we can begin
to gain a full understanding of the scope of our beliefs.

Approaches to Understanding Religion's Origins

I use this word "religion" for analysis purposes, here, in the
broadest sense: to mean any faith system. There are religions that
do not recognize the existence of a supernatural or transcendent
reality. People who understand religion as requiring a
connection with the transcendent will have to reexamine their

understanding for the rest of the book, for even these non-spiritual systems are built upon a faith foundation and that is their adherents' guiding faith.

One thing that can be helpful in understanding faith systems is knowing where they came from; because origin is the basis for direction. As there is no actual contemporaneous historical record describing the origin of any truly ancient belief system, we are dependent on the opinions of research anthropologists to develop theories about this topic. We must keep in mind, though, that in an ultimate sense, there is a way reality is structured, and the origin of that reality "is what it is." That doesn't change, no matter what theories are developed or what opinions are derived from them.

There is a huge problem that researchers run into, though. Since they don't have original records, they must create theories to organize the facts that they find so they can describe "origin" in its most-likely terms. And the theories they make depend upon the worldview beliefs they use to create them. Thus, any theory is only as fundamentally valid as the beliefs it is built upon – even before the acquired facts are applied to support (or refute) it! Exploring this topic at an academic level, all we can do is look at the possible theories and how the acquired facts support or refute them. It is different, though, when it comes to what we personally believe to be true. At that point, we have to look in another place.

As we explore this topic, we need to introduce one more element. This is another matter we will deal with more extensively later on, but it needs to at least be introduced here. As we look at the approaches to understanding the origins of religion, we need to note that there are only four worldview *categories*, and each one understands its approach to be the truth. The four worldview categories are: Naturalism, Animism, Far Eastern Thought, and Theism. With that introduction, let's look at the various theories concerning origins.

Natural Approach

The first category of theories we will look is the one based on Naturalism. A natural theory places the origin of religion in human society itself. It is based on the belief that there is no such thing as a supernatural reality, so religion has to have been man-made. The model primarily used to promote this point of view is an evolutionary model. Since there is only one worldview system that is naturalistic in nature, there is only one natural model category to look at.

> *"[There] are only four worldview categories, and each one understands its approach to be the truth. [They] are: Naturalism, Animism, Far Eastern Thought, and Theism."*

Evolutionary Model

An evolutionary approach begins with the assumption that the first form of religion that humans invented was very primitive. This theory asserts that over time, as human beings gained knowledge and experience, their beliefs also expanded to more complex forms.

One of the more prominent evolutionary models considers "Mana" to be the most primitive form of religion—the first form to exist. *Mana* refers to a "general awareness" of a spiritual force in the world.

As human societies developed and became more complex, naturalistic theoreticians believe that religious beliefs also became more complex. So based on this evolutionary approach, *Mana* naturally evolved into Animism—the belief that there are actual spirits in the spirit world that interact with the material world.

The next step in complexity, according to the evolutionary model, is Polytheism—where the spirits become more defined and turn into gods.

From there it evolves into Henotheism. This is the belief that there are many gods, but a particular group of people pick one and worship that one as their own.

Then comes Monotheism. This is the belief that there is only one God.

People who promote this evolutionary theory are generally those who do not believe in God, so they include one more level of evolution: Atheism. They believe the natural world is all that exists. So, when human beings advance scientifically to the point that they are able to understand the way the universe actually works, they can drop belief in God altogether.

Spiritual Approach

The other category of *models* begins with the belief that there is a part of reality (the "transcendent" part) that exists outside of the material universe. The other three foundational worldview systems, while their understandings of transcendence are very different, would each locate their belief about the origin of religion in that transcendent realm. So let's look at these spiritual models:

Original Monotheism Model

Original monotheism would be the choice of Theists. This approach begins with the belief that ultimate reality begins with God, who created the material universe from His location outside it. The assumption is that God created the material universe, placed human beings in it, and revealed Himself and His ways to them. Then, as the human population began to grow, various groups forgot about or put aside God's revelation; and began coming up with other ways to understand spiritual reality. In other words, the original belief about a single God was correct, but over time became corrupted; which led to the formation various false religions.

Original Animism Model

The original Animism model would be the approach of Animists, to whom, in truth, it would probably never occur to ask the question, "What is the origin of religion?" If they ever did ask this question, however, they would certainly start with their own beliefs.

Their starting point would necessarily be that actual reality consists of a universe that is divided into a material part and a spiritual part. In Animistic belief, the spirits in the spirit world and humans in the material world interact with each other in a symbiotic relationship. Animists would most certainly believe that all other belief systems began with this reality, then became corrupted and evolved into other beliefs as people spread out around the world.

> *"[There] are two categories of faith systems — worldview systems and belief systems. Worldview systems are foundational, and belief systems are based on the foundation of some worldview system."*

Original Far Eastern Thought Model

It seems likely that the original Far Eastern Thought model would be based on a thought process similar to the original Animism model. In this one, as well, it would probably never occur to believers in a Far Eastern Thought belief system to question the origin of religion. If they ever did take it up, however, they, too, would certainly begin with their own beliefs.

The starting point, though, would necessarily be that actual reality consists of an immaterial and impersonal transcendent reality, which spun off elements that became the material universe (which is both material and personal).

[Please note that in this analysis, the word "personal" means the possibility of creatures interacting in a personal manner or relationship. "Personal" implies self-awareness (self-consciousness), but also free-will. It is in contrast to "impersonal" which implies that none of these meanings or implications exist.]

The Far Eastern Thought belief is that the material universe is illusory. Based on this, believers in faith systems of the Far Eastern Thought category would, most certainly, affirm that all other belief systems began with their reality, then became corrupted and evolved into other beliefs as people spread out around the world.

Approaches to Understanding Faith Categories

As we move forward in our understanding of the concept of worldview, we need to take a moment and revisit a distinction we dealt with earlier. We noted before that there are two categories of faith systems—worldview systems and belief systems. Worldview systems are foundational, and belief systems are based on the foundation of some worldview system. The reason we need to make this distinction here is because, as we look at the different ways people approach the topic of worldview, making this distinction gives us the ability to organize our analysis with clarity.

Unfortunately, many of the approaches people use to try to explain worldview are somewhat baffling because they confuse worldview systems with belief systems. When an approach is used that incorporates this kind of confusion, our ability to make distinctions and comparisons between systems becomes blurred. But, let's look at the prominent ones:

"World Religions" Approach

One of the more common ways, perhaps even the most traditional way, of dealing with faith systems is to use a world religions approach. This entails simply listing the various belief systems in existence, side by side, then explaining their doctrines and practices. Typically, there is no attempt, nor even means, to categorize them for comparison with each other at a foundational level.

"Isms" Approach

Another approach to analyzing faith categories is to use an "isms" methodology. This is similar to the previous approach, but actually allows for worldview systems and belief systems to be looked at, to some degree, side by side. The problem we run into with this approach, however, is that we end up comparing apples and oranges in some cases. This is because some "isms" correspond more closely to certain worldview categories, while others correspond with particular belief systems. The drawback of this approach is that certain comparisons can be adequately made while others don't work so well.

"Selective Beliefs" Approach

Another approach is to simply pick and choose a handful of selected faith systems to compare. In one way this is like the "isms" approach, though it is limited by the particular faiths that are selected for comparison. For instance, if one were to try and include Christianity, Naturalism, Hinduism, and Marxism in his or her comparison, the result would be a system that included Naturalism as a worldview category, while the other three are belief systems which fit into a larger worldview class. This methodology runs into exactly the same problem as the "isms" approach. As such, the same problem exists here that existed with the "isms" method.

Worldview Approach

To avoid the problems associated with the previous approaches, we need to make a clear distinction between worldview and belief systems, then deal with them separately. James Sire pioneered this approach for the Christian community, and identified seven questions that define the outer limits of a worldview system:[1]

1. What is the nature of ultimate reality?
2. What is the nature of material reality?
3. What is a human being?
4. What happens to a person at death?
5. Why is it possible to know anything at all?
6. How do we know what is right and wrong?
7. What is the meaning of human history?

The approach used in this book takes Sire's method and attempts to simplify it even more. Instead of seven questions, we will use only three. The three questions do not leave anything out from Sire's list. Rather, the seven are folded into the three:

1. **What is the nature of ultimate reality?**
2. **What is a human being?**
3. **What is the ultimate a person can achieve in this life?**

Sire's questions 1 & 2 are folded into our question number one; questions 3, 5, and 6 are folded into our question two; and his questions 4 & 7 are tucked into our question three:

1. What is the nature of ultimate reality?
  1. What is the nature of ultimate reality?
  2. What is the nature of material reality?

2. What is a human being?
  3. What is a human being?
  5. Why is it possible to know anything at all?
  6. How do we know what is right and wrong?

---

1 *The Universe Next Door*—James Sire Intervarsity Press, Downers Grove, Illinois, 1979. In his 2009 5th edition, Sire proposes an eighth question: "What personal, life-orienting core commitments are consistent with this worldview?" which informs Chapter 21, below.

3. What is the ultimate a person can achieve in this life?
4. What happens to a person at death?
7. What is the meaning of human history?

So, with this, we are able to determine the line which cannot be violated that is distinctive to any given faith system (the *'are you in it or are you not'* line) by answering three simple questions. The answers to these three questions define the outer limits of EVERY faith system in existence—both worldview systems and belief systems. Since every system's outer limits are defined using the same questions, it becomes very easy to compare the different beliefs to one another—both at the worldview level and at the belief system level.

As we deal with the outer limits of worldview faith systems, we discover that every worldview literally contradicts every other worldview. In other words, each of the worldviews answer the three foundational questions in its own unique way. Belief systems also answer the three worldview questions, but there are some additional considerations when we deal with them: more on that later. For now though, let's look at the essential worldview questions to understand how faith systems are defined.

1. What Is the Nature of Ultimate Reality? (God)
Ultimate reality is defined as the most foundational concept about reality that could or does exist. It deals with such things as the existence and nature of God, transcendent reality, and the material universe. Every worldview has its own completely unique belief about what ultimate reality looks like.

2. What Is a Human Being? (Man)
Understanding the nature of a human being involves a

"[Each] of the worldviews answer the three foundational questions in its own unique way."

---

worldview's conclusion regarding all aspects of the human person—body, mind, and spirit. Every worldview has its own unique definition of a human being, as well as its own view about the nature of the human person as it relates to knowledge and morality. And as previously mentioned, every worldview belief literally contradicts every other worldview definition concerning this topic.

3. What Is the Ultimate a Person Can Achieve in this Life? (Salvation)
This final question digs into the personal meaning of life, and one's ultimate destination at death. Again, every worldview has its own belief about this topic, and every answer contradicts the beliefs of every other one.

The Exclusive Nature of Belief Systems

One of the most important points we must grasp about worldview systems is the exclusive nature of these systems. While many people like to think that what they believe is non-exclusive and open minded, nothing could be further from the truth. EVERY faith system in existence has a line that cannot be crossed and one still remain within that system: which makes every one of them exclusive and closed-minded. This line defines what can be accepted and what cannot. It is just that each system places the line in a different place.

I find it quite fascinating to hear people accuse Christians and Christianity of being narrow-minded. They typically make this charge because Christians make a point of expressing the notion that salvation is found ONLY in Jesus Christ. Well, the truth is, Christianity is narrow-minded in that way. Acceptance of Christ is the only way to salvation.

But this is not an expression of narrow-mindedness, it is an expression of truth. It represents the way reality is actually structured. It is a clear drawing of the line describing the boundary one cannot cross and still remain in Christianity.

Lest people think this is strange, though, it must be noted that those who accuse Christians of being narrow-minded are doing so based on their own beliefs about the limits of faith. In order to call Christians narrow-minded, they must evaluate Christianity based on limits that they are not willing to cross—in other words, based on their own narrow-minded point of view. We will look at this more fully going forward, but let's look briefly at where the four worldview categories are narrow-minded.

Naturalism—Naturalists will not accept any belief that acknowledges the possibility of a transcendent or supernatural reality.

Animism—Animists will not accept any belief that does not accept a transcendent reality which is symbiotically connected to the material universe: where spirits in the spirit world interact with humans in the material world.

Far Eastern Thought—Far Eastern Thought believers will not accept any belief that views ultimate reality as personal and material.

Theism—Theists will not accept any belief that denies the existence of God.

So, as you can see, narrow-mindedness and exclusivity are a part of EVERYONE'S belief system. It is just that the lines that define that exclusivity are drawn in different places.

How do we Understand Faith Systems?

There is a way reality is actually structured, and it is not structured in any other way. Interestingly, even the approach we use to look at this topic is based on what we believe about what is real. After all, we would not develop nor adhere to a theory about it based on beliefs we felt to be unreal. While it is not possible to step outside our personal belief system to create a credible explanation, it is helpful to understand the full scope of possibilities as we explore the topic. At the very least, this will help us make sense of the approach we are using. At the most, it will facilitate our quest to affirm the truth.

"There is a way reality is actually structured, and it is not structured in any other way."

Discussion Questions
1. What problems are associated with an evolutionary model of religious origins?
2. What problems are associated with an animistic model of religious origins?
3. What problems are associated with a Far Eastern Thought model of religious origins?
4. Why is a worldview approach to studying faith categories superior to any other method?

Consider this …

Ever heard of Kepler 444? Probably not. It is a star that is said to be 11.4 billion years old and has numerous planets circling it. Scientists don't believe any of its planets are habitable, but that does not keep astronomers from drooling over the thought that life exists on some planet somewhere else.

In an article in *Astrobiology Magazine* discussing Kepler 444,[2] astronomer Tiago Campante expressed the following sentiment. He wrote, "This system gives us hope that there are other habitable worlds that we can't detect because we don't have enough observing timespan yet." He continued, "Upcoming observatories could change that. Whether life can live for billions of years, however, is pure speculation."

There is no scientific evidence whatsoever that life exists outside of planet earth. However, this guy is so convinced that there is, he speculates about it in an article that really has nothing to do with life on other planets. How can that kind of mentality be explained?

Well, it is easily explained. Mr. Campante believes in a worldview system called Naturalism: based on that set of beliefs, since God does not exist, the only possibility for the emergence of life is by naturalistic evolution. Since he believes life "evolved" on earth, he is convinced that it has happened on other planets, as well. As a scientist, you would think he would require some kind of scientific evidence in order to believe that, but he doesn't. He believes it by faith and in spite of the fact that there is no science to back it up.

How is it possible for people to believe things that don't line up with what they say they believe?

2 *"Ancient Star Raises Prospects of Intelligent Life,"* May 7, 2015, Astrobiology Magazine (https://www.astrobio.net/).

Chapter IV

What is Worldview?
No, worldview is not simply how you view the world.

We have previously considered why an understanding of worldview is important, looked at some of the distinctions we need to understand about a worldview, and dealt with the parameters of worldview systems. Now, it is time to specifically define the concept.

One of the most fascinating aspects of a worldview relates to people's lack of knowledge of their own worldview foundation. Nearly everyone can tell you the doctrines they believe regarding their personal religious faith: but almost no one can do the same when it comes to the worldview foundation their faith is built upon. Worldview beliefs are so foundational to a person's understanding of reality that it is nearly impossible to conceive that other people could actually hold different worldview beliefs. As such, beliefs at that level tend to be unconscious. The only way to make these beliefs conscious is to deliberately study the topic.

Definition

Now that we have given some good background about worldview, it is time to finally define it. With this definition we can begin looking at the various worldview possibilities and compare them with one another.

> ***A worldview is a set of assumptions people hold about the nature of reality.***

"[An] assumption is nothing more than a belief that seems so obvious that it is difficult to imagine other people could believe something different."

At first glance, this definition may seem rather philosophical, academic, or even a little strange. But in truth, there is nothing more practical in people's lives than coming to understand their worldview. Everyone holds a set of beliefs about how reality is structured; and everyone lives life as if those beliefs are true— whether they are actually true or not. Let's break it down to the key ideas of this important concept.

The first key idea in the definition is the word "assumptions." A worldview is a set of *assumptions* about the nature of reality. In its essence, an assumption is nothing more than a belief that seems so obvious that it is difficult to imagine other people could believe something different.

The second key concept in the definition is expressed in the word "reality." When we think of how all of existence is structured, we are touching on what we mean when we use that word. The entirety of existence is structured in some actual way and is not structured in any other way. It is certainly possible to imagine non-actual structures, but no matter how creatively a non-real belief might be described, it does not change the way things actually exist.

Now that we have looked at the pieces, let's put it all together and see if we can grasp the full scope of the definition. A worldview is a set of beliefs (a faith position or set of assumptions) that is the organizing principle for an individual's understanding of how all of existence is structured and how it operates (*i.e.*, the nature of reality). A person's set of worldview beliefs may or may not align with the way reality is actually structured, but that is beside the point. Individual human beings have an incredible ability to live their lives, from birth to death, based on their own way of understanding reality, whether or not those beliefs are actually true.

> *"A worldview is a set of beliefs ... that is the organizing principle for an individual's understanding of how all of existence is structured and how it operates."*

Worldview Metaphors

The concept of worldview is an abstract idea. Because of that, it can be difficult for some to concretely understand what it is, or why it is important. As such, it is often a good idea, when we are dealing with abstract ideas like this, to use illustrations or metaphors to describe them. This can be particularly helpful when trying to understand worldview beliefs. We will now take a look at four different metaphors in order to give a clearer sense of what we mean by the term "worldview."

Environment

A worldview is like **a closed environment.** Consider a pond, for instance, and pretend that you are a fish living in the pond. Not only are you a fish, you are a scientist fish, and it is your responsibility to document everything that exists in the pond. You are familiar with all of the other kinds of fish that live there, as well as the snakes, mollusks, insects, plants, and everything else. You are also aware that something exists outside the pond, but know a very limited amount about it because you are not able to leave the pond. You can stick your head out of the water and see trees, grass, certain other kinds of plants, and even some animals which live around the pond. But as far as you know, the environment that surrounds you is all there is. There is nothing else.

However, imagine that one day you heard a loud splash and you swam over quickly to the place it came from, only to find a strange fish—one like you had never before seen. Being the curious sort that you are, you swam up to that fish and began asking him where he came from. He then began to tell you a tale about how he lived in another lake, was caught by a fisherman, brought to this new location, and thrown in. He then went on to describe other kinds of fish, water creatures, plants, and insects that you had never even known existed.

Having been totally confined to your own pond your entire life, there is no way for you to have known about any of the things the new fish was telling you. In fact, it seemed so fantastic that it was hard to believe what he was telling you was actually true. Yet, there he was. In truth, it is very difficult to imagine something existing that is so completely beyond one's own experience.

A worldview is **a belief environment.** Every person was raised in an environment that reflected the beliefs of those doing the raising. The worldview beliefs which were the underlying foundation in that environment were the default, and no one questioned them. In fact, no one considered that they could even be questioned: that is "just the way things are." As with the pond scenario, a worldview belief environment is never questioned, until something comes along from the outside and interjects another possibility.

Spectacles

A worldview is like **a pair of glasses.** Imagine that when you were born, your parents put a pair of goggles on your head that had red lenses. For your entire life, you had never seen anything without seeing it through those red lenses. In that case, the world seen through red-colored lenses would seem totally and completely normal to you. In fact, you would not even realize there was another possibility.

Suppose, though, that one day someone substituted clear lenses for your red ones. In that case, you would be seeing shades and colors the way they actually are, but it would not seem that way to you. In fact, it would seem abnormal. You would continue to consider it abnormal until some kind of explanation came along that was able to convince you otherwise.

A worldview is **a belief lens.** You evaluate everything in your life based on the worldview beliefs you learned growing up. If someone comes along and proposes a religious belief, a scientific theory, a view of history or gun control, or even a philosophy for raising children, that did not correspond with your worldview beliefs, it simply would not make sense and would seem wrong. These contrary ideas would continue to seem wrong until a different belief lens was explained to you in a way that made you think the new way represented reality.

Foundation

A worldview is like **the foundation of a building.** A building's foundation completely defines the potential for the use of a structure. You cannot build in ways that the foundation does not support.

First, it defines the shape of the building: you can only build the superstructure to the outer limits of the foundation. If you try to build outside the foundation, your building will crumble and fall very quickly in the places where the foundation does not exist.

Additionally, the foundation defines how you construct the building: you cannot build a twelve-story building on a foundation designed to hold only four. If you try to do that, the weight of the building will ultimately cause it to collapse.

A worldview is **a belief foundation.** It is an underlying set of beliefs that, while they are generally unconscious, support the conscious beliefs people think they live by. For instance, an underlying belief might be that God exists. If a person holds that belief, when someone tries to assert that the world could exist without God as the creator, the anti-God assertion would simply not make any sense because it stands outside the belief foundation. Likewise, if a person tries to somehow incorporate a belief that life on earth could have come about without the need for God's creative work, all the while still believing in God, those contradictory beliefs ultimately cannot not be supported by the foundation, and it will eventually crumble.

Language

A worldview is like **a language.** Virtually everyone communicates with other people using language. We have thoughts that we want to share with others, so we use sounds and symbols to communicate those ideas. The only problem is, there are many different languages; and people who try to communicate with others who don't speak their language don't have much success.

Suppose I walked up to you and said, *"Labrit."* In fact, you would understand the sentiment I expressed because that idea is not confined to a particular language. You can also express it in English. However, unless you understand the Latvian language, you probably would have no idea that I was telling you good morning. You know "good morning," but not knowing the Latvian language would keep you from understanding what I said.

A worldview is a belief language. If I express ideas to you based on a set of worldview beliefs that I hold, yet you adhere to a different worldview, you might understand the words I say but would not understand the meaning of the words.

Sometime back, I had a back-and-forth, Facebook conversation with a person concerning a YouTube video I posted about why I felt gay marriage was wrong. Parts of this conversation illustrate, perfectly, this point about not being able to understand concepts based on a different worldview foundation. The conversation went like this:

(Note: This Facebook conversation is quoted verbatim. Grammar and spelling mistakes have not been corrected.)

> *Meat:* What is wrong with gay marriage? Nothing. Pretty simple.
>
> *Freddy Davis:* Actually, the term gay marriage is nonsensical. The very definition of marriage requires a man and a woman. To take your point of view requires the redefinition of the word without any justification whatsoever. What you are really advocating is not marriage at all but the creation of a new way of defining family which has nothing to do with marriage.
>
> *Meat:* Ah, that old talking point. Yawn. From where are you getting this (supposedly) definitive, end all be all

"definition" of marriage? Lemme guess: the bible. The meanings of words and the practicing of social customs tend to change within a culture over time. You're afraid of change, apparently.

Freddy Davis: Ah, that old put down. Yawn. So where do you get your definition? Lemme guess: you made it up.

Meat: I recognize that dictionaries only describe the way that words are currently being used in a particular society; they don't prescribe the meanings of words as being set in stone. The meanings of words aren't like the laws of physics; they're malleable and open to change. Unlike your mind, apparently.

Freddy Davis: Either that, or you simply don't understand the concept of marriage. The problem is, as I stated before, you are trying to call something marriage that is actually something else. I don't know why you think you need to do that, but what you are advocating is simply not marriage.

Meat: No, you're just trying to appeal to the word "marriage" as if it some unaltering, unchangeable law of physics. It isn't. It's a social custom. Humans made it up. As such, humans can change it as they see fit.

Freddy Davis: Actually, you are trying to define reality in a way which assumes marriage is something different than what it is. The very concept of marriage involves a man and a woman. Your attempt to redefine it based on (gee, I don't even know what your basis is for trying to redefine it) has no basis in actual reality. Even if you change what is written in the dictionary you have not changed marriage. Marriage is what it is.

You can call a rock a piece of bread, too, but it doesn't change the fact that it is a rock.

Meat: Here you go again, trying to argue that marriage—which is, in actuality, a social custom invented by humans—is some sort of unchanging law of nature that we discovered, like the laws of thermodynamics or gravity. You're just appealing to your particular understanding of the word "marriage" and insisting that it's like Newton's laws of motion: unwaivering facts of nature. In reality, humans made this social custom up, just like all our other social customs. We invented the "rules" for it and each society defines those rules for themselves, if they even recognize the custom at all. As such, marriage is whatever we - the society practicing the custom - say it is.

Freddy Davis: I beg to differ. Marriage is not simply a social custom invented by humans. I would be interested to know what presuppositions you are using to make a statement like that. How do you know that "we invented the rules for it?" You are using an approach to understanding reality which has no basis in objective fact and are asserting it as if it does. If you are going to go down that road, you are going to have to back up your assertions (which you cannot do). You are simply in error. Marriage is an integral expression of the very nature of humanity and it exclusively involves a man and a woman. Attempting to change the definition does not change the reality.

Meat: Yes, marriage is plainly a social custom invented by humans, similar to funerary customs and rites of passage. That's why different cultures tend to have different rules for marriages, if they practice it at all, and those rules often change along with the social attitudes of the times. You have arranged marriages, child marriages, polygamous marriages, some cultures have allowed people to marry the "ghost" of a deceased loved one, sometimes divorces are allowed, sometimes not, etc, etc. The differences in how "marriage" is understood between different cultures, and the fact that these cultures often change those rules, is exactly what you'd expect from a man-made social institution. I'm guessing that you're going to try and argue along the lines of presuppositional apologetics. If marriage is such an "integral expression of the very nature of humanity", then why don't all people get married? Why do the rules vary from religion to religion, time period to time period and culture to culture? The only person here trying to make reality conform to their prior-existing beliefs is you. Not surprising from an evangelical presuppositionalist.

Freddy Davis: You are confusing marriage customs with marriage itself. You are making an assumption that they are the same. Also, the fact that you can come up with different words to hyphenate with the word marriage does not make your point. Marriage is the union of a man and a woman to create a social unit designed to build a family around which could then become the foundation for all other societal institutions. God instituted it and configured it to correspond with the biological composition of human beings as well as with man's spiritual nature. Your naturalistic presuppositions simply cannot be backed up. You have done nothing but make assertions without any kind of evidence whatsoever that what you are saying is truth - much less evidence which actually corresponds with your naturalistic presuppositions. Your argument simply does not hold together.

As you read this dialogue, isn't it interesting to note that we were both talking about the same topic. But because we came at it based on entirely different belief languages, it was almost impossible to come to a mutual understanding. The fact is, I did know his belief language and was able not only to challenge his beliefs but to counter them, as well. Beyond that, not only did he not understand my beliefs at a worldview level, he didn't even understand the implications of the beliefs he was asserting. He was making a worldview assumption that the material universe is all that exists. If the conversation had continued, I would have forced him to back up his beliefs—which he would not have been able to do.

The Seeming Reality of a Worldview

Before leaving this topic, I would like to reemphasize one particular point that is inherent in all of the metaphors: *A worldview is* **a paradigm for understanding how reality works; and people, typically, only understand their own paradigm.** People's worldviews seem real to them, literally; and anyone who doesn't believe what they believe appears to live in a fantasy world. Even with the conversation above, I have had Christians comment to me that they don't see how in the world Meat could possibly believe what he was saying. Yet, that is the point! He does believe it. Along with that, he believes that for me to believe what I expressed could only mean that I live in "la la land."

"[A] person's worldview seems absolutely real to them—whether it is real, in actuality, or not."

To illustrate this, let me share one more personal example. When

I lived in Okinawa, a man came into church exhibiting, what seemed to me, very strange behavior. He was waving his hand back and forth in front of his face and blowing air out of his mouth. I thought he was, perhaps, a bit mentally disturbed, but that was not the case at all. He was a very normal man. The pastor explained to me that he was a brand-new Christian who had come out of an animistic religious background. What I was witnessing was a "left-over" belief from his previous religion. He believed there were actual evil spirits floating around in the world. All he was trying to do was blow them out of the way so he would not run into any. Because he believed these evil spirits objectively existed, he was doing what would be normal and logical based on his beliefs.

It is important to grasp the concept that a person's worldview seems absolutely real to them—whether it is real, in actuality, or not. As such, when dealing with people who hold worldview beliefs that are different from your own, it is important to show respect, and be willing to take them seriously. This does not mean to accept their beliefs; but to realize they really do believe what they are saying. With that kind of respect for them as a person, it becomes possible to befriend and ultimately share with them a different way of understanding reality: the truth.

The Few and the Many

In a previous chapter we looked at the distinction between worldview systems and belief systems. While everyone holds worldview beliefs, these beliefs, as we saw earlier, are typically held at an unconscious level. We also saw that we have conscious beliefs that we refer to as "belief systems" that consist of the various religions, cults, and philosophies with which people around the world identify.

As we will see more fully as we move forward, there are a very limited number of worldview systems that exist in the world. In fact, based on the way we are dealing with them (in categories), there are only four. Worldview categories are very big-picture sets of assumptions about how reality is structured, and every religion, cult, and philosophy in existence is built upon one (or in some cases a combination) of these four. So, while there are only four worldview categories, there are scores of belief systems (some calculate them into the thousands).

Making the distinction between a worldview and a belief system is very important as we move forward. It allows us to analyze, compare, and contrast the faith systems that exist, and do it in ways that are not possible using other methods. It also allows us to analyze for truth.

Just the Beginning

Up to this point, we have only scratched the surface of what the topic of worldview has to offer us. We have only looked at definitions and distinctions that can help us understand the concept of worldview. As we move forward, we will get more specific, and actually identify and define the worldview categories themselves.

Discussion Questions

1. How would you define a worldview?
2. How is a worldview like an environment?
3. How is a worldview like spectacles?
4. How is a worldview like the foundation of a building?
5. How is a worldview like a language?

Consider this ...

What do you think? Is abortion okay or is it not? Is homosexual marriage a good thing or is it a bad thing? There are those who definitively answer one or both of these questions in the affirmative, and those who do the same in the negative. Then, of course, there are people who say there are some circumstances where it is okay, and other circumstances where it is not okay. So, who is right? These points of view are so exclusive that someone has to be right and someone has to be wrong (or at least partially wrong).

The different points of view all have their basis in the worldview beliefs of the individuals making the choices. It is impossible for all to be right because the points of view literally contradict one another. The different worldviews propose different ways of imagining what is real and what is not real. By understanding all of the possibilities, we have the ability to compare and contrast them in ways that help us discover the truth.

What are the possible ways to define reality?

Chapter V

What Are the Worldview Possibilities?
Are there really different ways reality is structured?

We have already looked at several important aspects of worldview. First, we noted that a worldview is a faith system: that is, every worldview rests on a faith foundation. We have also made the point that every worldview system represents a completely unique way of understanding how reality is organized. As a result, every worldview system ends up contradicting every other one. Additionally, we made the point that an understanding of worldview helps us grasp our own beliefs on a deeper level, as well as those of other people we interact with in life. Then, to understand the reason a worldview approach to understanding faith systems is so important, we looked at the concept of "essentials," we noted that there is a set of questions we can ask that defines the outer limits of every faith system. Based on those questions, we can directly compare one faith system to another.

The next step in the process of understanding worldview is grasping the tenets of the specific worldview systems themselves. We noted briefly that there are four basic worldview categories. Let's now begin learning the specific beliefs associated with each of them. The four worldviews are Naturalism, Animism, Far Eastern Thought, and Theism.

> *"[It] is impossible for more than one of these worldview systems to represent the way reality is actually structured."*

For the purpose of introduction, we will begin with a simple overview of the four worldviews. In the following chapters we will go into more detail about the specific doctrines and implications of each.

Naturalism

Naturalism is the belief that the only thing that exists is the material universe. There is no God or any other element of transcendent reality. Naturalists believe that empirical science can account for every aspect of reality.

Animism

Animism is the belief that all of reality is divided into two parts —the physical world and the spirit world. Animists believe that everything we see tangibly in the physical world belongs in that realm, and the spirit world is occupied by various spirit beings. The big-picture belief is that the two parts of reality interact with each other symbiotically. As such, what happens in one part has a direct effect on what goes on in the other part.

Far Eastern Thought

Far Eastern Thought is based on the belief that the material universe represents an illusory expression of reality, based on the fact that it is greatly separated from ultimate reality. This system asserts that the personal and material aspects of reality that we seem to experience in this world are actually not real. Rather, ultimate reality exists and operates in an entirely different way: it is seen to be an impersonal life force that exists beyond the material universe and has no material or personal element to it.

Theism

Theism is the belief that there exists a transcendent creator God who created the material universe and mankind for His own purposes.

Comparing the Worldviews

As we can deduce from these brief descriptions, each of the worldview systems have an entirely different way of understanding how reality is structured and organized. We can also see that they are so different, there is no way to reconcile the beliefs of one of them with any other one. It is impossible to believe God exists and doesn't exist at the same time. It is impossible for God to be personal and impersonal at the same time. It is impossible for there to be only one God and many gods/spirits at the same time. It is impossible for there to be a transcendent element to reality and no transcendent element to reality at the same time.

Because of these profound contradictions, it is impossible for more than one of these worldview systems to represent the way reality is actually structured. What that means is that there are literally billions of people in the world who live life based on a way of understanding reality that is simply not true. Later, we will do a deeper comparison and make some evaluations related to the search for truth. For now, though, just understanding the nature and structure of the worldview systems helps us get at the foundational beliefs of the many people who live in the world.

Discussion Questions

1. How would you define Naturalism?
2. How would you define Animism?
3. How would you define Far Eastern Thought?
4. How would you define Theism?

Consider this ...

There is nothing wrong with abortion.

There is nothing wrong with homosexuality.

There is nothing wrong with plural marriage.

There is nothing wrong with sexual relations outside of marriage.

There is nothing wrong with lying if it accomplishes your purposes.

There is nothing wrong with cheating—if you don't get caught.

In fact, there is nothing wrong with anything you want—as long as you have the power to protect yourself from those who might oppose you.

When there is no objectively-real, moral lawgiver, there is no objectively-real morality.

Why does Naturalism give people the right to create their own morality?

CHAPTER VI

The Naturalistic Worldview

YOU DID NOT COME FROM APES.

The basic premise of Naturalism is that there is no such thing as a supernatural existence. It asserts that the only thing that exists is matter, which is eternal and evolving. That is, all that exists is the physical universe, and the only laws that are operative in the universe, are natural physical laws. This is currently the dominant belief system in Western culture. It holds the greatest influence in the entertainment industry, the news media, the political arena and in the majority of educational institutions.

> *"Naturalism is currently the dominant belief system in Western culture."*

While Naturalism is expressed as a set of basic beliefs that cannot be violated, there are numerous belief systems that use it as a base, but go in different directions regarding other matters. Some of the most prominent forms of Naturalism include: Secular Humanism, Atheism, Agnosticism, Skepticism, Existentialism, Marxism, Positivism, and Postmodernism.

Naturalism and the Essentials

As we just saw, there are many different expressions of Naturalism. All of them, though, have the same essential foundation, and only differ regarding beliefs or emphases that relate to non-essential elements of the faith. The foundation is defined by how it answers the three essential worldview questions that were discussed in a previous chapter.

What Is the Nature of Ultimate Reality?

Naturalism asserts that there is no such thing as a supernatural existence. The natural universe is all that exists, and it operates strictly based on the natural laws of the universe.

What Is a Human Being?

Naturalists believe that human beings are nothing more than natural biological creatures that have evolved the largest and most complex brain of any in the animal kingdom.

What Is the Ultimate One Can Achieve in this Life? (Salvation)

On a macro level, Naturalism's view of salvation is that the most important thing for mankind is survival. On a personal level, salvation is merely the effort to achieve maximum personal pleasure and meaning in this life. There is nothing else.

"Since Naturalism only accepts that which can be demonstrated using observation and experience, ... the conclusions of naturalistic philosophy can't be demonstrated using empirical science."

Implications of Naturalism

As a worldview system, Naturalism is expressed, by Naturalists, in every part of life—without exception. Of course, they are no more consistent regarding their worldview than believers in any other system. That said, they do consider naturalistic beliefs to reflect the way reality is structured, and will attempt to live life as if it is true. The following explanations take several of the major categories of life and show how Naturalism deals with them.

Theology

Theology is the study of God. Since Naturalism begins with the belief that there is no such thing as a supernatural reality, its theology is merely the assertion of the nonexistence of God. With this approach to understanding reality, everything in all of existence must be accounted for based on the natural laws of the universe.

Philosophy (Reality, Knowledge, Values)

Philosophy is the study of reality, knowledge, and values; and explains these three subtopics by examining their nature, causes, and principles. Since Naturalism only accepts that which can be demonstrated using observation and experience, there is a problem when dealing with the topic of philosophy. The problem is that the conclusions of naturalistic philosophy can't be demonstrated using empirical science. It is based on logical reasoning rather than scientific methods. The problem here, for Naturalism, is that it begins with the foundational assumption that every part of reality can ultimately be understood based on the application of natural laws. But in this case, it does not use natural laws to come to its conclusions.

Unfortunately for Naturalists, none of the elements of philosophy can be demonstrated to be true based on naturalistic presuppositions. The best they can do is assert, by faith, that reality exists as a naturalistic construct, and one day we will understand how it all works.

Reality

Based on naturalistic presuppositions, naturalistic philosophy only considers the material universe to be objectively real. There can be nothing outside it. Accordingly, Naturalists believe that everything, in all of reality, operates according to natural laws.

Since Naturalists do not believe that an eternal mind exists beyond the material universe, they must base a naturalistic understanding of reality purely upon human reason. As such, any ideas that include belief in God are considered superstitious and unreal. This is expressed in the culture as a resistance to any kind of objectively real spiritual expression.

Knowledge

The origin of knowledge, based on naturalistic philosophy, rests on the evolutionary development of the human brain. Naturalists believe that the human brain has evolved to a high enough level of complexity for self-conscious thought to occur. As a result, the knowledge that humans are able to acquire has its origin in the brain's evolutionary development. They believe the brain is essentially a biological computer. Knowledge becomes possible as bits of information are acquired, stored, and accessed based on biological, electrical, and chemical functions within the brain.

Naturalists understand the concept of knowledge-based completely on a natural paradigm. It is expressed as:
   1. matter existed before mind,

2. humans evolved to their current state from less complex life forms,
3. design evolved out of chaos,
4. life emerged from non-life,
5. enlightenment (human understanding) emerged as an evolutionary product of brain development, and
6. all elements of reality emerged from chaos.

Naturalists believe human beings are purely physical creatures. As such, knowledge can only exist because of the operation of the human brain.

<u>Values</u>

Based on naturalistic philosophy, values are founded upon the belief that all of reality has its root in natural laws. Naturalists believe that human beings create values based on the needs of individuals and social groups. There is no God to reveal values from beyond the material universe, so human beings must develop all values themselves. Typically, they believe human beings develop values as a survival mechanism—which is considered to be a part of the evolutionary process. Humans choose appropriate values for their social groups based on what they perceive will give them the best chance of survival.

Naturalists believe that all values are derived from human reason, with survival being the ultimate goal. As such, they believe that all laws, and every other expression of morality within a society, are purely functional items. They do not believe there is any such thing as objectively real moral or immoral acts. Matters are considered wrong and bad if they work against the survival of the community. Anything beyond that is potentially acceptable.

"Naturalists ... believe that, by chance, human beings are the animal species that evolved a brain complex enough to become self-aware."

Anthropology

The word anthropology means the study of man. It is a social science that is concerned primarily with human culture, as well as the physical and social characteristics that create a culture.

Naturalistic anthropology understands human beings to be strictly biological creatures. Naturalists, then, evaluate every aspect of individual human life and social expression based on the principles of naturalistic evolution. They believe that, by chance, human beings are the animal species that evolved a brain complex enough to become self-aware. They do not believe in a God who could reveal proper morality, so the human animal must base all its actions on what it considers best for any given situation.

Naturalistic anthropology believes human social organization is the natural evolutionary expression of humanity's quest for survival. Naturalists consider that living in social groupings enhances the survivability of the species. For that reason, humans naturally form groups that develop their own unique cultural expressions.

Sociology

Sociology is the study of human social behavior. It is particularly focused on the origins, organization, institutions, and development of human society.

Naturalistic sociology is founded upon the worldview belief that there is no such thing as a supernatural reality. As such, mankind does not exist for any objective purpose: humans are merely animal creatures that have evolved from mindless matter, and will live until they meet physical death. Naturalists believe this evolutionary process developed in a way that caused human beings to be social animals as a means of survival. Since there is no overarching purpose for humanity, there is also, by extension, no purpose for society other than survival. Additionally, without a God to provide direction, there is no objective guidance for how society ought to be formed. A society can legitimately become whatever its citizens decide is right for them.

When it comes to actually developing societal rules (including moral rules), the struggle for physical survival becomes the most important value. As a society develops in the course of a group's evolution, it develops values, behaviors, and technology that will be useful for its survival.

"[Humans] are merely animal creatures that have evolved from mindless matter, and will live until they meet physical death."

Another implication is that since all of society's rules are made by the society itself, they can be changed whenever the group deems it to be helpful. If conditions or situations change, there is no compelling reason the cultural rules can't also be changed. Things that used to be considered wrong can become right, and vice versa, depending on the situation and desires of the people in the group. That change has nothing to do with innate morality, only with the desires of the group and the functionality of the change.

Psychology

The word "psychology" literally means the study of the soul. Psychology deals most specifically with the mind, mental states, and mental processes, and tries to discern how these interact with human behavior.

Psychology, in Naturalism, is based on the belief that human beings are purely physical animals with no spiritual part. Thus, the soul is nothing more than the physical self. This understanding leads to methods of dealing with the human mind and human behavior that are purely physiological. Using the common naturalistic approaches to psychology, curing human psychological problems is a matter of fixing wrong thinking by using behavioral techniques and medicines.

> *"[The] soul is nothing more than the physical self."*

Since Naturalism does not acknowledge the existence of a supernatural reality, all of the elements that people associate with the idea of soul are, necessarily, physical in nature. That is, the human sense of self-consciousness and free will are nothing more than the functioning of a physical brain; which has evolved to a level complex enough to give that illusion. As a result, naturalistic psychology involves learning techniques for manipulating the parts of the brain responsible for processing the emotional pain human beings experience in life.

One critical issue in naturalistic psychology involves discerning what makes up normal and abnormal psychological behavior. Since Naturalists don't recognize any kind of objective morality, they believe people must evaluate what is normal and abnormal based on what contributes to or breaks down a given societal grouping. Proper behavior, as is the case with proper morality, is relative to the situation and can change over time as circumstances change. The evaluation of right and wrong must be based on the contemporary beliefs of the majority in society, or the preferences of those who hold political power.

"... right and wrong must be based on the contemporary beliefs of the majority in society, or the preferences of those who hold political power."

In naturalistic thought, since society holds priority over the individual, what is morally appropriate is whatever society holds to be acceptable. As such, the source of psychological conflict arises out of issues that have their root in societal morality rather than offense to God.

In naturalistic psychology, mental suffering is considered the enemy. Naturalists identify psychological issues by observing what causes mental pain within individuals. Success in dealing with these occurs when the distress is eliminated.

The work of trained counselors, then, is the work of socialization. Naturalists believe that individuals are helped as they learn to accept and live in harmony with society's rules. By reconciling people's thoughts to the standards of society, they are able to eliminate internal conflict. Since Naturalists believe all remedies are physiological, they think they can generate psychological cures using medication or behavioral techniques designed to help people change their way of thinking.

"[The] capacity for self-consciousness and free will can only be the result of naturalistic evolution."

Communication

Communication deals with the way human beings convey meaning to one another. Since, from a naturalistic perspective, communication begins with the belief that human beings are strictly material animals, the capacity for self-consciousness and free will can only be the result of naturalistic evolution. Naturalists believe the human brain has evolved to the place where this kind of information processing is possible. There are debates among Naturalists as to whether this capability is actual or is merely an illusion based on evolutionary brain development. In any case, having these capabilities allow human

"Since there is no God, there is no external moral law giver. Thus, human beings must determine right and wrong based on local circumstances ... personal preferences of individuals and social groups, or on what is seen to be useful for the survival of the species."

beings to produce thoughts that they are able to communicate to other persons who have that same capability.

Ethics and Morality

Naturalism asserts that there is no such thing as an objective right or wrong, good or evil. Since there is no God, there is no external moral law giver. Thus, human beings must determine right and wrong based on local circumstances. Since there is no external basis for morality, the foundation for developing a moral code is relegated to one of two possibilities: it must either be based on the personal preferences of individuals and social groups, or on what is seen to be useful for the survival of the species.

In Naturalistic thought, morality also has a particular character. When a culture creates values and norms, these are understood to be strictly functional elements. Since there is nothing to give anything or any being innate value, there can be nothing innately good or bad, right or wrong about any process, object, or belief. An individual or group determines the goodness or rightness of a thing or process based on personal preference, or its usefulness as a survival mechanism.

Finally, since there are bound to be different opinions as to which specific moral rules should hold sway over a society, the only way to definitively settle the issue is by wielding power. The individual or group that has the ability to control a society is the one that gets to set the moral rules. The final result is played out by means of the law of the jungle—the survival of the fittest.

Biology (Origins, Evolution/Variety, Value of life)

The topic of biology relates to the study of life or living matter.

More specifically, it deals with life's origin, growth, reproduction, structure, and behavior.

Based on a naturalistic view of biology, everything must be naturally explainable. As such, life itself must have originated by natural means. While there is no experimental scientific basis for this assumption, Naturalists recognize no other possibility: it must be that **inert chemicals combined under the right circumstances to produce life.**

> *"Based on a naturalistic view of biology, everything must be naturally explainable."*

Origins

Based on a naturalistic point of view, the only possibility for the origin of life is that it emerged naturally. Belief in a supernatural genesis is considered superstitious and unscientific. As such, for Naturalists, **teaching anything in educational institutions other than a naturalistic approach to origins is considered taboo.**

Evolution/Variety of Life

The same is true when attempting to account for the variety of life forms on earth. Since Naturalists acknowledge no supernatural existence, they only accept a naturalistic approach to explaining the variety of life forms on earth. Since Darwinian evolution is the only theory available to make this case for Naturalism, **Naturalists believe it should be the only approach schools are allowed to teach.** For them, it is not relevant that no actual biological mechanism has ever been scientifically demonstrated to allow for this kind of evolution to occur. It is a fixed article of the faith that a naturalistic approach is all that is possible.

Value of Life

Since Naturalists believe no supernatural reality exists, there is no possibility of an objective purpose for life. Life is valuable simply because it exists. Additionally, all life has naturally and purposelessly evolved from less complex forms. **As such, human life is not innately more valuable than any other life form**. This leads to the understanding that the value of life focuses on the survival of the species, rather than the fulfillment of a purpose for individuals.

As such, determining whether or not taking a life is acceptable must be based on how it affects the survival of the society, not on any kind of objective morality. The result of this kind of thinking is that murder, abortion, and euthanasia may or may not be legitimate options depending on the particular situation. If society believes taking an individual life contributes to the survival of the species, it can be seen as good thing.

In general, the survival of an individual life is less important than the survival of society. When it comes to ending life, those in positions of power determine rightness or wrongness as they evaluate the benefit to the social order. This principle applies both in the private and the public arena.

It also extends beyond the life of human beings. Since no life form is more important than any other, some Naturalists also find it important to advocate for other life forms—which becomes the basis for animal rights and environmental activism.

Law

The topic of law relates to the particular rules society uses to promote order within the culture. A naturalistic view of law is expressed in the principle of positive law. Law from this worldview perspective has no objective or supernatural basis. Rather, it is established on the perceived needs of society and/or the personal inclinations of those in power. No other possibility is acknowledged. And, since there is no objective foundation for law, laws themselves, and even the foundational principles for interpreting law, can be changed anytime based on contemporary circumstances.

> *"Law from this worldview perspective ... is established on the perceived needs of society and/or the personal inclinations of those in power."*

Using this belief as a basis for understanding law, Naturalists do not recognize a constitutional document to be unchanging based on the intent of the writers. Rather, it is subject to changing interpretations based on contemporary societal circumstances and the views of those responsible for interpreting.

As Naturalists believe there is no God, no one is left but man to invent law and create order in society. This must be done based on the beliefs of those who have the power to impose their will. The result is a system of laws that can be ever changing based on the whims of society and the personal preferences of those in power.

Naturalistic legal systems tend to put the highest value either on the desires of the ones wielding power or on the perceived needs of society in general. In either case, the rights of the individual fall below the needs of the collective.

Politics

Politics relates to the practice of administrating states or other political units. It is the management of a governmental system.

Naturalistic politics is based on the notion of a purely secular government. This is established upon a worldview foundation that does not recognize the existence of a supernatural power or purpose. As such, politics is necessarily focused completely on an earthly outcome, which promotes the ultimate goal of the natural order—the survival of the species.

The stress, again, is on the interests of the collective over that of the individual. Since a communal mentality is the governing principle of society, politics is best expressed through some type of collectivist political form. The most popular collectivist approaches in our current time include, progressivism, socialism, and communism. Some type of dictatorship is also a possible political expression of a naturalistic approach.

> *"Naturalistic politics is ... necessarily focused completely on an earthly outcome, which promotes the ultimate goal of the natural order–the survival of the species."*

Since Naturalists do not believe there is any such thing as objective morality, the only restraints political leaders have on their power is that which is placed on them by the pressures of society or by their political competitors. They are, thus, free to exercise all of the political power they can manage to accumulate for themselves.

Those who agree with this kind of political philosophy do not see this to be a problem as long as the politicians exercise their power to promote the survival of the society. As Naturalists don't believe in the existence of any kind of objective morality, the means used to govern are not subject to an objective moral code. What is permissible is only constrained by what the population will allow.

Also, submission to government authority by the individual is considered of ultimate value. It is the governing authorities who ultimately determine the boundaries of what is morally acceptable. As such, it is the rigid duty of those within society to obey the government in order to promote the smooth operation and ultimate survival of society. Those who disobey rightly deserve to receive the full discipline of government power.

"Naturalists believe the only principles that exist to guide economics are those which society's leaders consider to be helpful in advancing the goals of human society."

Economics

Economics is the study of the production, distribution, and consumption of goods and services within a society. It also deals with the attempt to understand economic systems and how to manage them effectively.

Naturalistic economics operates on the principle of interventionism. A naturalistic understanding of economics begins with the belief that there is no supernatural existence. As a result, Naturalists believe the only principles that exist to guide economics are those which society's leaders consider to be helpful in advancing the goals of human society. Based on naturalistic thought, the species (society), rather than the individual, takes precedence. The tendency that emerges is an economic approach that promotes the welfare of society above that of the individual. This generally involves some kind of central guidance by those who control the purse strings of society.

There is also a tendency among some who adhere to Naturalistic economics to believe that social justice demands everyone share limited resources equally. That is, no matter how much or how little an individual produces, everyone should end up with the same amount. It is considered that "this is only fair." As such, there should be no rich and poor. Everyone gets the same.

Based on the concept of social justice, wherever one finds a society with a poor lower class, Naturalists believe the poverty occurred because the rich have exploited the poor. As such, the poor don't have a chance because the rich keep them down. A redistributive model of economics overcomes this problem by taking the wealth of the better off and redistributing it to the less fortunate by manipulating tax rates, or through tax breaks and government programs. Of course, this principle does not apply to the ones who are in positions of authority.

History

History is the study of past events. Contained within this topic is an understanding of the purpose of human existence.

"[History] has no meaning beyond that which is assigned by human beings."

Based on naturalistic beliefs, history has no meaning beyond that which is assigned by human beings. It must be that way because they do not believe there is any supernatural being above history who is able to assign a higher purpose. History becomes simply a record of the natural operation of the material universe. Naturalists see humans as progressing to higher levels through history, but this is strictly the result of evolutionary progression as a natural animal.

Naturalists also understand history to be linear, in that it moves from past to present to future in a non-repetitive fashion. However, they see no overarching purpose associated with it since no one exists to give it a purpose.

Education

Education has two important components. First, it is the process of conveying specific knowledge and skills to others. Second, it involves imparting good judgment and wisdom. The goal is to pass the important elements of culture from generation to generation.

Education is a lifelong process; beginning at birth and continuing throughout life. It involves both formal and informal elements. Formal education is generally associated with participation in some

"[Education's] primary function is to promote the survival of the human race in the here and now."

kind of educational institution, while informal education is what people learn from other parts of life.

Naturalistic education is based on the belief that there is no transcendent reality. As such, education's primary function is to promote the survival of the human race in the here and now. Naturalists believe that man is a chance accident of naturalistic evolution, so no objective purpose exists for any part of human existence, including education. As with the development of every other aspect of human culture, Naturalists hold that education is merely a useful tool for societal development and survival. Thus, the purpose of naturalistic education is to provide the collective with the skilled personnel it needs to promote survival. Based on naturalistic worldview beliefs, there is no compelling reason any particular person must advance their level of education. The educational advancement of any particular individual is of little consequence.

A Summary of Naturalism

As a worldview system, Naturalism asserts that all of reality can be accounted for within the natural universe and by the natural laws which order it. It asserts that there is no such thing as a supernatural existence. As such, every part of life must be able to be accounted for and explained based on the natural operation of the world. Thus, when studying and dealing with the various elements that make up the operation of human life, it must be done in a way that provides a natural explanation.

> *"Naturalism asserts that all of reality can be accounted for within the natural universe and by the natural laws which order it."*

Discussion Questions

1. What is the most basic premise of Naturalism?
2. How do Naturalists deal with the three essential worldview questions?
3. Why do you think Naturalists tend to be hostile to Christians?
4. Pick one of the following topics and explain how Naturalism would deal with it: Theology, Philosophy, Anthropology, Sociology, Psychology, Communication, Ethics and Morality, Biology, Law, Politics, Economics, History, and Education.

Consider this ...

At the time it was released, 20th Century Fox's 2009 movie *Avatar* became the biggest blockbuster movie of all time. One of its primary appeals was that it took 3D technology to a whole new level. To me, the movie was fascinating for a different reason. If a person really wants to understand a set of worldview beliefs at a visceral level, it is necessary to be able to actually feel what it would be like believing—living out—that worldview. Because of the way the film writers made the Animists to be the sympathetic characters in the movie, and because they portrayed an Animistic worldview "as if" it was true, it gave the viewer the ability to feel what that worldview would be like.

In the movie, the "good guys" are the Na'vi people who live on the planet Pandora. The Na'vi are Animists who worship the mother goddess, Eywa.

To solve an energy problem, humans traveled to the planet in order to mine an important energy source. In the process of it all, they attack the Na'vi. Of course, in the end, the Na'vi people, along with the planet's animals and the nature spirits, defeat the bad humans.

Movies have a way of allowing people to identify with characters in a way that lets them feel what the sympathetic character feels. Avatar does that by causing viewers to identify with characters who are living an animistic worldview.

What is it about Animism that prevents people from being truly creative?

Chapter VII

The Animistic Worldview

Animism's Basics

A nimism is a worldview system that acknowledges many gods/spirits that are functionally interactive with the material universe. The various belief systems within Animism have different ways they think about how the spirits express themselves, but they all begin with the same basic premise. In general terms, Animists believe that there are spirits associated with all different parts of the material universe. Some are seen to inhabit material objects (like trees and rocks), some are heavenly objects (sky, sun, moon, stars), some are animals, and others are the spirits of people who have died and passed into the spirit world.

Animism believes that these spirit beings interact in a symbiotic relationship with beings in the material world. In practical terms, the work of humans is to offer prayers and offerings in order to meet the needs of the spirit beings in the spirit world. If this is done properly, the spirits will cause good to happen to the individuals in the material world. This works the other way, as well: if the humans don't do the right things, the spirit beings

> *"Animism believes that ... spirit beings interact in a symbiotic relationship with beings in the material world."*

will cause bad things to happen.

While Animism is expressed as a set of basic beliefs that cannot be violated, there are numerous belief systems that use it as a base but go in different directions regarding other matters. Some of the more prominent forms of Animism include:

- Japanese Shinto,
- Traditional African Religions,
- Witchcraft/Wicca,
- European Paganism,
- Astrology,
- Fortunetelling,
- Spiritism,
- Voodoo/Santeria, and
- Native American Religions.

Animism and the Essentials

While there are many different expressions of Animism, all of them possess the same essential foundation and only differ regarding the details of how they are expressed in life. The foundation is defined by how it answers the three essential worldview questions that were discussed previously.

What Is the Nature of Ultimate Reality?

Concerning ultimate reality, Animists believe that everything in existence is symbiotically connected. They understand reality to be divided into two parts—the physical and the spiritual. What goes on in one part directly affects the beings that dwell in the other. Every being has a responsibility to help keep the system in balance. They must, therefore, be diligent in taking care of their responsibilities related to the smooth operation of the whole.

What Is a Human Being?

Animists regard humans as responsible beings who dwell in the physical part of reality: responsible for performing various rites and rituals that meet the needs of the spirits in the spirit world. It is believed that by doing this well, individuals can not only avoid the negative consequences of not fulfilling their obligations, but can also actually manipulate the gods/spirits to cause good things to happen to them. It is generally believed that when individuals die in the physical world, they become spirits in the spirit world.

What Is the Ultimate One Can Achieve in this Life? (Salvation)

Regarding the ultimate a person can achieve in life, Animists believe that the most important thing an individual can strive for is to take care of the obligations that keep the spirit beings satisfied. In doing this, they believe that the spirits will bless and take care of them. They hold that this not only affects the individual, but family and society, as well.

Implications of Animism

As a worldview system, Animism gets expressed, by believers, in every part of life —without exception. Animists consider animistic beliefs to reflect the way reality is structured and attempt to live life as if it is true. The following explanations take several of the major categories of life and show how Animism deals with them.

"Animism believes that there exist many gods/spirits in the spirit world that symbiotically interact with the beings in the material world."

Theology

Theology is the study of God. Animism believes that there exist many gods/spirits in the spirit world that symbiotically interact with the beings in the material world. Since Animism begins with the belief that there is a symbiotic connection between the material and the spirit worlds, each part must take care of its responsibilities within its own realm to keep the universe properly balanced. With this approach to understanding reality, Animists do not generally look to solve personal or societal problems based on innovation and technology. Instead, they try to discern what gods/spirits are troubled, and attempt to make that right.

Philosophy (Reality, Knowledge, Values)

Philosophy is the study of reality, knowledge, and values. People address these three topics by examining their nature, causes, and principles. As such, those who study philosophy must use logical reasoning to come to their conclusions. This can be somewhat problematic in Animism as Animists typically do not understand, downplay, or even dismiss certain elements regarding reality that are necessary for one to deal with the topic of philosophy. In Animism, the foundational principles associated with every part of life tend to be centered on the activity of the gods/spirits, often actually excluding the operation of known natural laws. As such, an entire segment of the operation of natural reality is simply not acknowledged to exist. Animistic philosophy, therefore, is not able to get a handle on many parts of reality.

Reality

Based on its animistic presuppositions, philosophy must be grounded in the concept that all of reality is symbiotically

> # *"In Animism, the foundational principles associated with every part of life tend to be centered on the activity of the gods/spirits, often actually excluding the operation of known natural laws."*

connected. While both the spirit and material worlds are considered objectively real, the powers that influence the operation of the universe cannot be objectively understood. That is true because they believe the execution of these powers originate in a transcendent realm that humans have no way of directly understanding or controlling.

Since Animists downplay the ability of the intellect to understand the operation of the material world, they must receive their understanding of its operation from a different place. Their source is tradition. They believe the ancestors gained understanding of what needs to be done to appease and placate the spirits—mostly through trial and error—and passed that knowledge down through the generations.

Knowledge

The origin of knowledge, based on animistic philosophy, is not a topic that Animists would typically consider. They generally just accept that the universe exists the way we experience it, which includes the existence of human beings. Of course, there are some animistic traditions that posit a creation, but even in those places the teaching about creation is done using mythical stories. This is not a method that will, generally, account for the personal characteristics of God or of man.

The result is that Animists simply observe what exists and assume it has always been that way. They make no attempt at all to understand it. Thus, the knowledge that humans hold simply exists. There is no reason for it. It is just there.

Animists understand the concept of knowledge based partially on a paradigm that uses human observation as its basis. It is expressed as:

- mind and matter have always existed,
- gods/spirits existed before humanity,
- design was created by the gods/spirits,
- life emerged from life,
- enlightenment (human understanding) emerged from trial and error, and
- all elements of reality reflect order.

Values

Based on animistic philosophy, right values are believed to be an innate element of the universe. Human beings, through the ages, simply discovered them as they lived their daily lives. As people live and participate in life activities, when things go well, Animists note what seems to have caused it. The same is true for when things go badly. Over many generations, they observe the patterns and create traditions that seem to take advantage of the things that cause good, and avoid things that seem to cause bad. The activities that cause these things are then attributed to what pleases or displeases the spirits. When they think they

"Animistic anthropology understands human beings to be material creatures with a spiritual core."

understand these matters, the values associated with them are codified in the society.

Anthropology

The word anthropology means the study of man. It is a social science that is concerned primarily with human culture, along with the physical and social characteristics that create a culture.

Animistic anthropology understands human beings to be material creatures with a spiritual core. As such, Animists, evaluate every aspect of individual human life and social expression based on the idea that human beings are connected with the spirit world, and that human life cannot be disconnected from the spirits in the spirit world. They believe the actions people take in life have an effect on the spirits in the spirit world. These spirits have the ability to cause problems if the humans do not live rightly. As such, human beings must live life in a way that maintains the balance between life in the material world and the spirit world.

Animistic anthropology largely believes human social organization centers around the family and clan. Spirits in a particular locale are typically connected with particular families and clans, so the social structure serves to maintain those relationships.

Sociology

Sociology is the study of human social behavior. It is particularly focused on the origins, organization, institutions, and development of human society.

Animistic sociology is founded upon the worldview belief that the spirits in the spirit world need to be taken care of by the activities of the humans in the material world. An important part of this relates to maintaining relationships across the entire material-spiritual spectrum. This involves clans, tribes, and families maintaining their proper relationships with each other: with all of them minding the transcendent relationships with the ancestors and other spirit beings, as well. This provides a social structure that takes into account all of the relationships within society across time. Animists believe these relationships do not change over time, as they reflect the way reality, in general, is structured.

When it comes to actually developing societal rules (including moral rules), the means for doing that is, basically, trial and error. As people live life, they discern what causes good and bad things to happen in their lives individually and in the society as a whole. The things that cause good are considered moral and right, while the things that cause bad are considered immoral and wrong. Over time, even generations, people learn these things, and this becomes the standard for understanding morality. When people do things that either detract from or promote the smooth operation of reality, the spirits let people know by causing bad or good to happen.

"An important part of this relates to maintaining relationships across the entire material-spiritual spectrum."

Psychology

The word "psychology" literally means the study of the soul. Psychology deals most specifically with the mind, mental states, and mental processes; and tries to discern how these interact with human behavior.

"Animists ... think of the soul based on its interaction with the spirits in the spirit world."

Psychology is not generally a topic that will be under discussion in Animism, but, obviously, there is a way that Animists live life that involves mental states and processes. Since Animists consider humans to be spiritual beings housed in a physical body, the concept of "soul" does exist. The soul, though, is not necessarily thought of in individual terms as we see in Theism. Rather, they think of the soul based on its interaction with the spirits in the spirit world. They do not generally think in terms of where the soul will go after death, they simply assume it will go to the spirit world.

The concern regarding the soul in daily life, however, has more to do with how one thinks and acts in order to maintain proper balance in the entirety of the universe. This leads to a way of thinking that is more concerned with the entirety of reality than with personal matters. Thus, free will and self-consciousness, while exercised in daily life, are not matters of concern. The focus is more on the collective as it exists in both the material and spiritual parts of reality. Also, in Animistic psychology, psychological problems in humans are quite likely to be evaluated as some kind of action taken by the spirits in response to deeds done by humans.

Communication

Communication relates to the way human beings

> "[Communication] takes place between human beings [and] involves interactions with spirits in the spiritual realm."

convey meaning to one another. From an animistic perspective, communication is not something that only takes place between human beings. It also involves interactions with spirits in the spiritual realm.

"Animists believe that ethics and morality ... emerge as actions that reflect the smooth operation of the universe."

Ethics and Morality

Animists believe that ethics and morality are expressions of the ongoing operation of reality. However, they are not based in philosophical beliefs, but emerge as actions that reflect the smooth operation of the universe. Animists believe that every creature, in all parts of reality, must fulfill their responsibility in order to make sure that the totality of reality operates smoothly. They believe that when people neglect their proper role, bad things happen. The actions that cause bad things are the basis for understanding immorality; while actions that promote harmony become the definition of right morality.

Biology (Origins, Evolution/Variety, Value of life)

The topic of biology relates to the study of life, or living matter. More specifically, it is concerned with life's origin, growth, reproduction, structure, and behavior.

"An animistic view of biology takes everything at face value."

An animistic view of biology takes everything at face value. There is no attempt to study life and living things using a scientific perspective. Animists only feel it necessary to recognize that life exists and that it is symbiotically related to the spirit world.

Origins

There is no single animistic viewpoint regarding the origin of life. Generally, in animistic groups, the origin of life is expressed using mythological tales. Each group would typically have its own story.

Evolution/Variety of Life

Animists don't generally consider the reason for the existence of the variety of life forms on earth. They simply recognize their existence and seek to understand how that fits into the circle of life.

Value of Life

Animists have a high regard for life, human and other animals, because they believe all of life is symbiotically connected. What happens with one life form affects all other life forms.
As such, taking a life can be acceptable if it helps maintain balance in the universe—for instance to help sustain the lives of others. That said, they generally see wanton taking of life to be a bad thing, as it breaks down the proper operation of the universe.

Law

The topic of law relates to the particular rules society uses to promote order within the culture. An animistic view of law is based on how people view the operation of reality in the universe as a whole. Animists see the universe operating in a particular way, and all of life must be conformed to that way. Otherwise, bad things will begin happening to people individually, as well as to others who are related in some way. If people begin taking actions which break down the harmony that exists in the universe, bad things will happen. Laws, then, reflect their perception of what creates harmony. Societal rules reflect not only the actions people take in the material universe, but also how they interact with the spirit world.

Politics

Politics involves the practice of administrating states or other political units. It is the management of a governmental system. Animistic politics is generally exercised in the context of a family, tribe, or clan, since animistic societies are typically comprised of those kinds of groupings. As such, the people who ascend to leadership are usually the natural leaders of those groups—an elder or, perhaps, someone from a royal family.

"Animistic politics is generally exercised in the context of a family, tribe, or clan, since animistic societies are typically comprised of those kinds of groupings."

The focus of leadership in these societies is stability based on the natural operation of the universe. Thus, leaders do not tend to manage their positions based on the desire to gain and maintain power. Rather, they exercise their role in a way that keeps people focused on fulfilling their obligations—toward other people and toward the spirits.

Economics

Economics is the study of the production, distribution, and consumption of goods and services within a society. It also attempts to understand economic systems and how to manage them effectively.

Animistic economics generally operates on a principle of shared resources. It begins with the belief that no one can own nature, and every being is a co-participant in it. As a result, Animists believe the main principle that guides economics has to do with people simply using the resources necessary for survival, and maintaining balance in the universe.

"Animists believe the main principle that guides economics has to do with people simply using the resources necessary for survival, and maintaining balance in the universe."

History

History is the study of past events. Contained in this is an understanding of the purpose of human existence.

In Animism, history and tradition actually become the authority source for their very understanding of reality. People learn what is right and wrong in the process of living daily life and as they observe the results of the actions they take. Right becomes associated with what produces good results for the family or tribe, and wrong associated with what produces bad results.

This knowledge is noted and passed on to the rest of the people in the society, and ultimately from generation to generation. In this way, they are able to gain the knowledge needed to live in harmony with all of the various parts of the universe.

While purpose is inherent in the process, Animists typically don't think in those kinds of categories. The universe simply exists, and it is and it is up to human beings to accommodate themselves to its operation. History is generally remembered in terms of stories that help pass on the knowledge needed to live life properly.

Education

Education has two important components. First, it is the process of conveying specific knowledge and skills to others. Second, it involves imparting good judgment and wisdom. The goal is to pass the important elements of culture from generation to generation.

Education is a lifelong process beginning at birth and continuing throughout life. It involves both formal and informal elements. Formal education is generally associated with participation in some kind of educational institution, while informal education is what people learn from other parts of life.

> "In Animism, history and tradition actually become the authority source for their very understanding of reality."

Animistic education is typically not based on a sense that there is a need for any kind of formal education. Children simply learn as they live life in the community and out in nature. They learn how to properly interact with the spirits, and what they need to know regarding basic survival skills, by the direct teaching of parents and others in the society.

A Summary of Animism

As a worldview system, Animism asserts that all of reality exists in a single realm that is divided into a material and a spiritual part. The two parts interact with each other in a symbiotic relationship, and each part must operate in ways that maintain balance.

Animism is a worldview that has not been very prominent in modern American history. It has, however, gained a significant amount of traction in recent years as fascination with and acceptance of unusual and esoteric faiths has increased. The implications of Animism in life are expressed in several areas.

"Animistic education is typically not based on a sense that there is a need for any kind of formal education. Children simply learn as they live life in the community and out in nature."

First, in Animism, the world, and life in general, are not seen to be moving toward a higher destination. Basically, everything is focused on the present. As a result, the tendency of Animists is to simply live life one day at a time and accept things the way they are. Whenever something "bad" happens, they assume that it is the work of an offended spirit. That being the case, the remedy to the problem is not to find some technological or educational process to solve it. Rather, it is to discover which spirit/deity has been offended, then offer prayers and offerings to salve its anger.

The impact on culture from this approach to life is that there is no built-in inner drive to strive toward higher levels of technological and other cultural achievement—either individually or as a society. As a result, purely animistic cultures tend to see very little technological or educational advancement over the period of extended generations.

Discussion Questions
1. What is the most basic premise of Animism?
2. How do Animists deal with the three essential worldview questions?
3. What would you expect Animists to think about Christianity and why?
4. Pick one of the following topics and explain how Animism would deal with it: Theology, Philosophy, Anthropology, Sociology, Psychology, Communication, Ethics and Morality, Biology, Law, Politics, Economics, History, and Education.

"Animism asserts that all of reality exists in a single realm that is divided into a material and a spiritual part ... interacting ... in a symbiotic relationship, and each ... [operating] in ways that maintain balance."

Consider this ...

When considering the Far Eastern Thought worldview, many people think almost exclusively of Hinduism or Buddhism. But this worldview system can be found in some very American places, as well. For instance, Christian Science is a belief system based neither on the Christian faith nor on science. It has its roots in the Far Eastern Thought worldview.

Christian Scientists begin with the notion that there is no personal God. They believe he/it is nothing more than "infinite mind," and matter is an illusion and doesn't exist. Thus, human beings also don't exist as material creatures: they are exclusively spiritual beings. The material nature of humanity is considered to be an illusion.

While Christian Science is not a Far Eastern Thought belief system in the strictest sense of the word, their belief in the illusory nature of the material universe was influenced by it. These Far Eastern Thought concepts have actually found their way into all kinds of prominent beliefs in the West, such as New Age and the Unity Religion. These ideas are also prominent in many movies and TV shows. Because it does show up in so many parts of the pop culture, it is a good idea to have a solid grasp of the Far Eastern Thought worldview.

What is it about Far Eastern thought-that causes people to be satisfied with their lot in life?

CHAPTER VIII

The Far Eastern Thought Worldview
MAY THE FORCE BE WITH YOU—NOT!

Far Eastern Thought Basics

F ar Eastern Thought originated, and is most prominent, in the Far East—hence the name. A more technical description would be pantheistic monism.

Pantheism is commonly described as a belief that god is everything and everything is god. That is, there is no distinction between the secular and the divine. In considering this definition, though, it is important to note that the use of the word "god" is not meant to imply that a personal creator exists. In Far Eastern Thought, transcendent reality is understood to exist, but it is essentially impersonal, not personal. There is no god capable of hearing, responding, revealing, or interacting in any way with mankind.

Monism is the belief that all of reality is composed of, and reducible to, a single substance. That is, everything that exists is made up of the same substance and only appears as different things because that essential substance is able to take different forms. In the Far Eastern Thought worldview system, that most basic substance is an impersonal life force that is constantly moving toward unity. As mentioned above, that essential reality is impersonal and there is considered to be no personal God.

Of all the worldview systems, this one is generally the most difficult for Westerners to grasp because its approach to

---

"Of all the worldview systems, this one is generally the most difficult for Westerners to grasp because its approach to understanding reality is so different from Western worldview foundations."

---

understanding reality is so different from Western worldview foundations. Far Eastern Thought begins with the belief that there is a mass of impersonal life force which exists in a place that transcends (exists outside of) material reality. Based on the operation of that transcendent reality, pieces of the life force have spun off to a location far enough away from the main body that it has taken on a different appearance. While ultimate reality is understood to be impersonal and immaterial, that part which has spun off—what we perceive to be the material universe—has taken on the appearance of being material and personal. As human beings are a part of the material universe, their perception of reality is material and personal: however, even that is understood to be an illusion.

It is believed, though, that the part that spun off is not destined to remain in that separated state. In fact, these pieces of the life force are understood to be constantly working their way back toward the main body of the impersonal life force, with the ultimate goal being to re-merge with it.

All life forms in the physical universe are believed to be nothing more than pieces of the impersonal life force that have been encapsulated in some kind of physical body: each one beginning as a lower life form. When a life form dies, the piece of the life force that animated its body remains and reincarnates to a higher life form. Thus, the lower the life form, the further it has to go to re-merge with the main body. Over many lifetimes, the life form reincarnates to higher and higher levels, until it finally reaches the highest stage. At that point, it is able to escape the reincarnation cycle and re-merge with the main body of the life force.

The power that moves the life form forward in its reincarnations is karma. As a creature lives its life, it accumulates either good or bad karma: good karma is gained by living life properly, and bad karma by living life improperly. The amount of good karma gained in a lifetime determines how rapidly the life force advances.

There are some important implications regarding life for those who adhere to a Far Eastern Thought system. The primary impact of Far Eastern Thought on culture is to promote passivism. This passivism, however, is not simply related to how individuals relate to conflict. Rather, it is associated with the very essence of how one thinks about the structure of reality.

The material world is understood to be an illusion. This does not mean illusory in the sense of not existing, but that nothing that goes on in the material universe relates to matters of ultimate significance. Nothing that humans experience in this life is understood to be a true expression of reality. The purpose of this life is to gain enough good karma in the current incarnation to move to a higher level in the next. The

> *"The purpose of this life is to gain enough good karma in the current incarnation to move to a higher level in the next."*

particular individual accomplishments achieved in any given incarnation really do not mean much, except to help one move forward on the path.

The ultimate expression of passivism, then, is to sit back and accept the life one has been born into. If it is at a low level, this must simply be accepted, and the individual must do his or her best in it in order to incarnate at a higher level in the next life. If one is born at a higher level, the goal is the same.

As such, there is no point in struggling to accomplish anything beyond the level of one's current incarnation. People should do the best they can with their current life. The purpose is not to create a better physical life; it is to gain a higher level in the next incarnation.

While Far Eastern Thought is expressed as a set of basic beliefs that cannot be violated, there are numerous belief systems that use it as a base but go in different directions regarding other matters. Some of the more prominent forms of Far Eastern Thought include: Hinduism, Hare Krishna, Transcendental Meditation, Buddhism, Taoism, Jainism, and Sikhism.

Far Eastern Thought and the Essentials

While there are many different expressions of Far Eastern Thought, all of them have the same essential foundation. These various expressions only differ regarding the details of how they are expressed in life.

What Is the Nature of Ultimate Reality?

In Far Eastern Thought, ultimate reality consists of an impersonal life force. This life force is both impersonal and immaterial. The material universe is believed to contain elements of that life force that are separated from the main body; working their way back toward unity through successive material incarnations.

What Is a Human Being?

Mankind is understood to be an expression of the impersonal life force that has been successively reincarnated and has finally reached the human level. When the life force reaches the highest human stage, it becomes possible for it to escape the cycles of reincarnation and re-merge with the main body of the impersonal life force.

What Is the Ultimate One Can Achieve in this Life? (Salvation)

As for salvation, the goal of life is to ultimately merge with the main body of the impersonal life force. It is believed that one must live rightly in one's current incarnation to accumulate good karma to make progress on that journey.

Implications of Far Eastern Thought

Theology

Theology is the study of God. Far Eastern Thought begins with the belief that there is such a thing as a transcendent supernatural reality, but it is impersonal in nature. As such, all of reality, while having life as a part of its make-up, operates in a mechanical fashion with no personality to guide it. The concept of God does not exist in the sense that Theists think of Him.

"The concept of God does not exist in the sense that Theists think of Him."

There is, therefore, no reason why the material universe exists. It is simply a function of the blind operation of ultimate reality.

Philosophy (Reality, Knowledge, Values)

Philosophy is the study of reality, knowledge, and values, and attempts to understand these three topics by examining their nature, causes, and principles. As such, those who study philosophy based on Far Eastern Thought worldview presuppositions have a bit of a problem. For Far Eastern

---

"For Far Eastern Thought, the understanding of reality is completely immaterial and impersonal."

Thought, the understanding of reality is completely immaterial and impersonal. With that as a starting point, the personal evaluations that must be made about what goes on in the material universe, including philosophical arguments, are necessarily illusory. They are not seen to express the true nature of ultimate reality.

Unfortunately for Far Eastern Thought believers, assertions about reality, knowledge, and values cannot be objectively dealt with based on natural explanations. Since the natural universe does not express the true nature of ultimate reality, any evaluations made about it cannot be objectively known. The best Far Eastern Thought adherents can do is assert what they believe without having the ability to give any kind of objective evidence those beliefs are true.

Reality

Based on Far Eastern Thought presuppositions, the material

universe is considered to be illusory. Since ultimate reality is immaterial and the natural universe is material, what we are able to interact with is only the illusion. Accordingly, it is impossible for Far Eastern Thought believers to say anything definitive about it.

Since Far Eastern Thought believers do not believe that an eternal mind exists, they must base their understanding of reality purely upon human experience. They believe that even though they can't reason their way to understanding, they can experience their way there. Unfortunately, there is no way to demonstrate that this is true, as there is no way to arbitrate between various ways people say they experience reality.

Knowledge

The origin of knowledge, based on Far Eastern Thought philosophy, also has no material basis. There is a belief that it is somehow possible to know things about reality by disengaging the mind and gaining some kind of experience of it outside of human intellectual perceptions. However, there is no explanation as to how this could be true—especially since all of our evaluations are experienced within, and based upon, our material lives. It is simply believed based on the presuppositions of the worldview.

Obviously, as they live their lives in the material world, people who believe this worldview do possess knowledge and use it in the course of living life. But they believe the knowledge has no use or benefit beyond its function in the material world. In ultimate reality, which is understood to be impersonal, knowledge, as a concept, simply does not exist.

Far Eastern Thought believers understand the notion of knowledge based exclusively on human experience.

It is expressed as:
1.   there is no ultimate mind, and matter is an illusion,
2.   transcendent reality existed before humanity,
3.   material reality arose out of the operation of a larger transcendent reality,
4.   life emerged from the life force,
5.   enlightenment (human understanding) emerged from human experience, and
6.   all elements of material reality are illusory.

Values

Based on Far Eastern Thought philosophy, values are founded upon karma and have no meaning in an ultimate sense. Values only pertain to the material world where human beings seem to experience life as personal and material. In human experience in the material world, good values are those that allow one to accumulate good karma. Bad values are the ones that cause the accumulation of bad karma. But as we consider this truth, we must note that the very concept of karma, itself, only has meaning in the illusory material world. Once the pieces of the life force are able to escape the illusory material universe, they are all combined and exist in a state that is impersonal and immaterial. In that circumstance, the very concept of values is meaningless.

Anthropology

The word anthropology means the study of man. It is a social science that is concerned primarily with human culture, along with the physical and social characteristics that create a culture.

In Far Eastern Thought, its anthropology understands human beings to be illusory expressions of an impersonal life force. Its understanding is that pieces of the impersonal life force have spun away from the main body and settled far enough away from it that it is expressed in material and personal ways—contrary to its essential essence. Far Eastern Thought adherents believe that every living thing is essentially a vessel for the piece of the impersonal life force that animates it. That piece of the impersonal life force is believed to continually reincarnate as it moves toward ultimately escaping the material universe and reconnecting with the main body of the life force in its transcendent existence.

"[Human] beings simply represent the higher-level stages of the reincarnation process potentially within a few reincarnation cycles of making that escape from the material universe."

In Far Eastern Thought, human beings simply represent the higher-level stages of the reincarnation process. As such, humans are potentially within a few reincarnation cycles of making that escape from the material universe.

Since ultimate reality is immaterial and impersonal, nothing has actual meaning: an understanding of meaning requires personality.

The fact that human beings must live life in the material world does not change ultimate reality. It only means that we must live with the illusion of meaning while we live on earth.

Far Eastern Thought anthropology believes human social

organization exists based on the concept of karma. That is, as the many pieces of the life force continually reincarnate, karma creates a kind of pattern in the world that is expressed in the societies of the creatures that are reincarnating. There is no ultimate meaning in these societies as meaning requires self-conscious purpose, and ultimate reality is impersonal and without any form of consciousness. Ultimately, in this life, it is up to human beings to align, to the highest degree possible, with the way karma is being expressed. This allows the life force to continue the reincarnation process in the most efficient way possible.

Sociology

Sociology is the study of human social behavior. It is particularly focused on the origins, organization, institutions, and development of human society.

In Far Eastern Thought, sociology is founded upon the worldview belief that human life and human society are determined, at any given time, by the operation of karma. As life forms move through the reincarnation process, they end up where they are based on the accumulated karma from previous lifetimes. As such, human societies emerge as they are supposed to at any given time.

There is also a particular order within the societal system. In the process of reincarnating through various lifetimes, societies are naturally ordered in the way they should exist. Individuals are born into the situation that is proper for them based on karma. This creates a natural ordering of society that people should accept. They will naturally move to higher levels in future lifetimes if they live their current life in ways that accumulate good karma.

As such, societal rules (including moral rules), are fixed based on karma. People need to accept their status in life and live within that status as best they can.

"[Societal] rules (including moral rules), are fixed based on karma. People need to accept their status in life and live within that status as best they can."

Psychology

The word "psychology" literally means the study of the soul. Psychology deals most specifically with the mind, mental states and mental processes, and tries to discern how these interact with human behavior.

Psychology in Far Eastern Thought is based on the belief that the ultimate reality of human essence is impersonal. In fact, the essence of all life is the impersonal life force. Thus, in the grand scheme of things, everything that appears to be personal in human life is actually an illusion. Since humanity must live the current life in this world, human beings must deal with the personal things that happen. In the end, though, since ultimate reality is actually impersonal, the things we perceive as personal are meaningless.

This understanding leads to methods of dealing with the human mind and human behavior in ways that put a premium on discounting the things related to material life. Thus, rather than attempting to cure this life's ills, the approach of human psychology is simply to accept things the way they are.

"[Methods deal] with the human mind and human behavior in ways that put a premium on discounting the things related to material life."

Belief in karma is the foundation for this kind of thinking. The belief is that individuals are born into their current life based on the accumulated karma of previous lives. Furthermore, when this life is over, they will be reincarnated into the next life based partially on the karma accumulated in this life. For the purpose of accumulating good karma, human beings should accept where they are and do their best in their current situation. This allows them to ultimately get to the place where they can altogether escape the material universe with its many problems.

Communication

Communication pertains to the way human beings convey meaning to one another. Since, from a Far Eastern Thought perspective, communication begins with the belief that the essence of human life is completely impersonal, the illusion that is communication does not have any kind of ultimate meaning. It may be useful for living life in one's current incarnation, but there is no ultimate significance. As such, communication should be used to help one accumulate good karma, in order to promote advancement in the next incarnation. Other than that, it has no real significance.

> *"[Communication] does not have any kind of ultimate meaning."*

Ethics and Morality

Far Eastern Thought bases its entire understanding of morality on the idea of karma. Since ultimate reality is absolutely impersonal, there can be no such thing as objectively real moral beliefs—particularly since moral beliefs have a personal foundation.

That said, there is an impersonal basis for morality in the karmic system. There are things which cause a life form to accumulate good karma and promote its advancement through successive incarnations. Those things are, by default, considered the basis for good morality. By the same token, things which cause a life form to accumulate bad karma are, by default, morally bad.

That said, the basis for good and bad morality is not right and wrong in the sense of doing good or bad deeds. Far Eastern Thought does not accept that there is any kind of personal transcendent being in existence capable of

> *"Morality is strictly based on doing the things that affect one's karma."*

defining good and bad deeds. Morality is strictly based on doing the things that affect one's karma.

The biggest problem in dealing with this topic relates to defining what helps one accumulate karma. Since there is no personal transcendent being capable of sharing information on this topic, human beings must somehow discern through other means what promotes the karma. There are ancient writings that share this kind of information, but we are still left with the problem concerning how those writers came up with their thoughts. It is a problem without a viable solution.

Biology (Origins, Evolution/Variety, Value of life)

The topic of biology relates to the study of life or living matter. More specifically, it deals with life's origin, growth, reproduction, structure, and behavior.

"As the material universe is not believed to be an expression of actual reality, the study of [Biology] can only be useful as a "this-worldly" exercise."

Based on a Far Eastern Thought view of biology, biological science has no ultimate significance. As the material universe is not believed to be an expression of actual reality, the study of biology can only be useful as a "this-worldly" exercise. While there is literally no objective basis for this assumption, Far Eastern Thought believers can support no other possibility.

Origins

Based on a Far Eastern Thought point of view, life is an expression of the transcendent impersonal life force. The origin of life is believed to exist in the eternal mass of life force that exists beyond the material universe. Parts of this life force spun off from the main body and ended up far enough away that it has taken on the illusion of being material and personal. This personal and material expression, though, does not represent ultimate reality. While there is no objective basis for this belief, that is not a problem based on the beliefs of the worldview.

Variety of Life

The variety of life forms on earth are accounted for based on karma and reincarnation. As a living thing lives its life, it accumulates karma which will cause it to become a different life form in its next incarnation. The fact that there are so many pieces of the impersonal life force that are all working their way to continually higher levels accounts for the many life forms in existence on the earth.

Value of Life

Life for Far Eastern Thought believers is not something to value, it is simply something that exists. And the material and personal expression it takes in the natural universe is not even its true form. Ultimate reality is a life force, but it is totally impersonal. As such, there is, in the ultimate sense, nothing to value and no one to value it. Any feeling of value people have is, in the ultimate sense, illusory.

Law

The topic of law relates to the particular rules society uses to promote order within the culture. A Far Eastern Thought view of law is based on the concept of karma. The ultimate goal of the pieces of the life force that are currently in the material part of reality is to, through successive incarnations, escape the material world and reconnect with the main body of the life force in the transcendent world. That happens as it accumulates good karma in the course of its many reincarnation cycles.

As it relates to morality, the things a life form does which allow for the accumulation of good karma is what is considered moral, and that which causes bad karma is immoral. Applying that

> *"As it relates to morality, the things a life form does which allow for the accumulation of good karma is what is considered moral, and that which causes bad karma is immoral."*

principle to the legal framework that exists in the material world, the things which cause good karma should be legal and that which causes bad karma should be made illegal. It is only a matter, then, of determining what those things are and codifying them into the legal system.

Politics

Politics involves the practice of administrating states or other political units. It is the management of a governmental system. Far Eastern Thought politics is also based on the notion of karma. According to this worldview concept, individuals are reincarnated each time into the station in life they are supposed to be in based on karma from their previous lives. It is considered that the political class represents a stage in the reincarnation process, so people are born into it as a result of prior accumulated karma.

> *"[In] Far Eastern Thought, the political class represents a stage in the reincarnation process, so people are born into it as a result of prior accumulated karma."*

The stress, then, is on promoting the kind of society where the normal operation of karma can do its work. In the end, there is no meaning in the process, as ultimate reality is totally impersonal. That said, there is the mechanical operation of the material world that must take place; and an orderly environment that allows karma to work properly is considered important.

Economics

Economics is the study of the production, distribution, and consumption of goods and services within a society. It also deals with the attempt to understand economic systems and how to manage them effectively.

As with so many of the other topics we have dealt with, Far Eastern Thought economics also operates based on the principle of karma. Here, it is important to realize that people are born into the social class they are supposed to be in based on accumulated karma from previous lives.

"[The] economic situation is the result of how karma is expressed in the lives of those who are born into the places that control the economy."

By the same token, the economic situation that exists in the world is the result of how karma is expressed in the lives of those who are born into the places that control the economy. As with politics, there is no personal reason why things are the way they are: it is all a result of the action of karma. Thus, the goal of those controlling the economy should simply be to create an environment that allows people to accumulate good karma during their lifetime.

From the consumer side, since every person is in the place in the reincarnation cycle that they were meant to be, all should be content in their station in life.

History

History is the study of past events. Contained within this topic is an understanding of the purpose of human existence.

Based on Far Eastern Thought beliefs, history has no ultimate meaning. For there to be meaning, there must be someone to express meaning. Ultimate

> *"Based on Far Eastern Thought beliefs, history has no ultimate meaning. Time moves in cycles, not from past to present to future."*

reality, however, is impersonal. Because of that, there can be no ultimate meaning for anything. And since the pieces of the life force in the universe are expressions of the ultimate life force, the sense people have on earth of the material and personal are necessarily illusions.

Beyond that, the Far Eastern Thought understanding of time is not linear, but cyclical. In other words, there is no such thing as history in the way humans typically understand it. Time moves in cycles, not from past to present to future.

Education

Education has two important components. First, it is the process of conveying specific knowledge and skills to others. Second, it involves imparting good judgment and wisdom. The goal is to pass on the important elements of culture from generation to generation.

Education is a lifelong process that begins at birth and continues throughout the rest of one's physical life; and involves both formal and informal elements. Formal education is generally associated with participation in some kind of educational institution, while informal education is what people learn from other parts of life.

Far Eastern Thought education is understood to be based on the outworking of karma in the reincarnation process. Based on karma, people are born, in any given incarnation, in the place they are supposed to be born. That being the case, the life situation dictates what place education should play in a given life. In order to accumulate good karma for the future, it is incumbent upon every individual to understand their place in life and do what they should in that life.

> *"[Education] is understood to be based on the outworking of karma in the reincarnation process."*

There is no ultimate meaning to education since ultimate reality is impersonal. As such, it only has meaning in the context of an individual's current incarnation. In the ultimate sense, the very idea that consciousness exists, which affords the possibility of true education, must be considered an illusion.

A Summary of Far Eastern Thought

As a worldview system, Far Eastern Thought believes that ultimate reality is both immaterial and impersonal. The natural universe and everything in it objectively exist, but in a form that

> "As a worldview system, Far Eastern Thought believes that ultimate reality is both immaterial and impersonal."

is material and personal and does not reflect the ultimate reality it came from. As such, all of existence within material reality is illusory. The pieces of the life force that were spun off of the transcendent main body of life force are, through successive reincarnations and based on the principle of karma, working their way back to ultimately rejoin the main body.

Discussion Questions

1. What is the most basic premise of the Far Eastern thought worldview?
2. How do Far Eastern Thought believers understand the three essential worldview questions?
3. What would you expect Far Eastern Thought believers to think about Christianity and why?
4. Pick one of the following topics and explain how Far Eastern Thought would deal with it: Theology, Philosophy, Anthropology, Sociology, Psychology, Communication, Ethics and Morality, Biology, Law, Politics, Economics, History, and Education.

Consider this ...

People who believe in God think of Him in various ways, with a song as a good expression mode. For Christians, God is eternal, personal, and the One who gives life meaning as the Christian praise song, *Alpha and Omega*,[1] describes God from the Bible.

> *He is Alpha and Omega, The beginning and the end*
> *He's behind me, He's before me, He's ever my friend*
> *Whatever I do, wherever I go, Jesus is my source and my goal.*
> *You are Alpha and Omega, The beginning and the end*
> *You're behind me, You're before me, You're ever my friend*
> *Whatever I do, wherever I go, You are my source and my goal.*

In the Muslim song, *God Only Knows*,[2] we find a Muslim image of what Islam thinks of Allah.

> *Only God knows how much, My heart and soul have melted within you.*
> *Only God knows how much, My heart and soul have melted within you.*
> *This is the one whose eyes weakened me, I swear.*
> *What's inside of me? Only God knows.*
> *This is the one whose eyes weakened me, I swear.*
> *What's inside of me? Only God knows.*

This song praises a God who is transcendent and knows all, but who does not interact with humans on a personal level. So, "only God knows" what is truly going on in a person's life and He controls all.

Theism ix not a monolithic worldview, so, a clear understanding of its category members is necessary to finding the nature of reality.

If Theism is true, how can a person hold theistic beliefs yet be completely wrong?

---

1 *He is Alpha and Omega* - A W Weber/S S Powell © 1977 Sparrow Song
2 *God Only Knows* (El Alem Allah—Original in Arabic) by Amr Diab

Chapter IX

Theism's Basics

Theism is the belief that there is an objectively real, infinite, and transcendent God who is responsible for creating and sustaining the material universe. Based on this worldview system, God is generally understood to be a person, though of a higher order than humanity. For the most part, Theistic groups depend on some kind of revelation to support their position. They understand this to be possible because, as a person, God is able to communicate instructions to mankind. It is up to humans, then, to receive and follow this revelation in order to please God.

There are many different forms of Theism which look to different kinds of revelation, and which understand the character and desires of God in very different ways. The common thread in Theism is not that they all view God the same (or the *same* God, for that matter), but that they all understand reality to be structured in the same basic manner.

"Theism is the belief that there is an objectively real, infinite, and transcendent God who is responsible for creating and sustaining the material universe."

While Theism is expressed as a set of basic beliefs that cannot be violated, there are numerous belief systems that use it as a base but go in quite different directions regarding other matters. Some of the more prominent forms of Theism include: Christianity, The Way International, The Unity School of Christianity, Children of God, Jehovah's Witnesses, Mormonism, Judaism, and Islam.

Theism and the Essentials

While there are many different expressions of Theism, all of them have the same essential foundation. They only differ regarding the details of how they are expressed in their doctrinal positions.

What Is the Nature of Ultimate Reality?

Concerning ultimate reality, all Theists believe that there is an actual, infinite, and transcendent God, who is the Creator and Sustainer of the physical universe. Theists believe there is a spiritual part of reality located outside the physical universe where God exists.

What Is a Human Being?

In Theism, mankind is understood to be a special creation of God. Man's purpose is to discern the purpose of God and live it out in this life. Upon physical death, it is believed that individuals will enter the part of the spiritual world that is appropriate based on how life was lived on earth.

What Is the Ultimate One Can Achieve in this Life? (Salvation)

As for salvation, Theism affirms that the purpose of life is to discern the will of God and live it out on earth. Doing so faithfully will allow a person to enter eternity with God.

Implications of Theism

Theology

Theology is the study of God. Since Theism begins with the belief that God exists, theology becomes not only a central theme, but the very starting point for understanding a theistic worldview. With this approach to understanding reality, a grasp of the nature and ways of God provides an explanation of origins, the character of man, and the means for understanding salvation.

> *"Since Theism begins with the belief that God exists, theology becomes not only a central theme, but the very starting point for understanding a theistic worldview."*

Philosophy (Reality, Knowledge, Values)

Philosophy is the study of reality, knowledge, and values, and digs into these three topics by examining their nature, causes and principles. As such, those who study philosophy based on theistic worldview presuppositions must understand the way God exists and how He created the world to operate. Since Theists believe in the existence of God, they must also believe that He is able to somehow communicate His will and His ways

> *"... philosophy based on theistic worldview presuppositions must understand the way God exists and how He created the world to operate."*

to mankind. It is through this revelation that true knowledge and appropriate values can be known.

While every theistic belief system will deal with the topic of philosophy in the same basic manner, the conclusions reached by each will be quite different. The reason for this is because the source of revelation for each one is different—that is, the particular God the different religions worship is different. Thus, the specific teachings about reality, knowledge, and values will be different.

Reality

Based on theistic presuppositions, philosophy looks to a transcendent source for its ultimate understanding. There is generally a belief that the material universe operates based on fixed natural laws set in place by God. At the same time, they recognize that there exists a part of reality beyond the material universe that is not bound by the natural laws of the physical universe. As God was the creator of the natural universe, Theists believe that He is capable of interacting with His creation without disrupting its operation.

Knowledge

The origin of knowledge, based on theistic philosophy, is God Himself. Theists believe that knowledge originated with God, and that He created human beings with the capacity to gain and use knowledge. As a result, humans can acquire and use knowledge of the natural universe as they interact with the world. There is also the belief that it is possible to gain knowledge of the part of reality that exists beyond the material universe: where God exists. That knowledge, however, must be revealed by God Himself. Since God is an objectively real person who has communicated with mankind using propositional revelation (human language), it is possible for some transcendent knowledge to be known.

Theists understand the concept of knowledge based partially on a natural paradigm and partially from revelation. It is expressed as:

- mind existed before matter,
- God existed before humanity,
- design existed before creation,
- life emerged from life,
- enlightenment (human understanding) emerged from light (God's revelation), and
- all elements of reality reflect order.

Values

Based on theistic philosophy, values are founded upon the nature and will of God. Theists believe that God has established the world to operate in a particular way. He then used various means to reveal that to humanity. It is His revelation that explains what is right and wrong, and it is up to humanity to discern and live by that revelation. By living according to these revealed values, mankind is able to please God.

"Theistic anthropology understands human beings to be persons created by God for His own purposes."

Anthropology

The word anthropology means the study of man. It is a social science that is concerned primarily with human culture, and the physical and social characteristics that create a culture.

Theistic anthropology understands human beings to be persons created by God for His own purposes. Theists, then, evaluate human actions in light of God's revelation to man.

Accordingly, theistic anthropology believes human social organization has been established based on the natural order of the creation. Accordingly, humans should live life in that context based on what God has revealed.

Sociology

Sociology is the study of human social behavior. It is particularly focused on the origins, organization, institutions, and development of human society.

> *"... human beings exist for a specific purpose, and God has revealed that purpose."*

Theistic sociology is founded upon the worldview belief that God created mankind in a particular way to serve His purposes. As such, human beings exist for a specific purpose, and God has revealed that purpose. Humans should, thus, learn God's purpose from His revelation, then organize society and live life based upon it.

When it comes to actually developing societal rules (including moral rules), God's revelation is seen to be its source. As a society develops, it is incumbent upon the group to base its values, behaviors, and technology on that revelation.

Another implication is that since all of society's rules are based on an objective revelation from God, there is an unchanging quality to them.

- In some cases, this would relate to the particular societal rules themselves.
- In other cases, the relationship is connected more to the principles that the rules should be based upon.

Psychology

The word "psychology" literally means the study of the soul. Psychology specifically addresses the mind, mental states, and mental processes—and tries to discern how these interact with human behavior.

Psychology, in Theism, is based upon the belief that human beings are persons created by God who have the ability to act based on free will and self-determination. In Theistic systems the soul is more than the physical self: it contains a spiritual element that is also capable of somehow interacting with

> *"... the soul is more than the physical self: it contains a spiritual element that is also capable of somehow interacting with God."*

God. This understanding leads to methods of dealing with the human mind and human behavior, that extend beyond the purely physiological.

> *"Psychological problems ..., are rooted in issues of rebellion against God, and can only be overcome by solving those rebellion issues."*

Psychological problems, in Theistic belief systems, are rooted in issues of rebellion against God, and can only be overcome by solving those rebellion issues. Depending on the particular belief system, this generally means discovering the things a person is doing wrong based on God's revelation and correcting them. These things are understood based on the revelation God has given to humanity.

The work of psychology, then, is essentially a spiritual exercise. As people discern the things that disturb the soul and get those straightened out, they resolve psychological issues.

Communication

Communication deals with the way "persons" convey meaning to one another. From a theistic perspective, communication begins with the belief that human beings, as persons created by God, are created with the capacity for self-consciousness and free will. As such, the communication that takes place between persons is essentially a spiritual process.

"Since God has determined what is right and revealed it to mankind, it is essential that human beings discern what that is and live by it."

Ethics and Morality

Theism asserts that there is such a thing as an objective right and wrong, good and evil. This morality is specifically defined by God and revealed to humanity. Since God has determined what is right and revealed it to mankind, it is essential that human beings discern what that is and live by it.

Biology (Origins, Evolution/Variety, Value of life)

The topic of biology relates to the study of life, or living matter. More specifically, it addresses life's origin, growth, reproduction, structure, and behavior.

"A theistic view of biology asserts that all of physical life operates in a natural environment based on natural laws, but the origin of life itself was based on the creative hand of God."

A theistic view of biology asserts that all of physical life operates in a natural environment based on natural laws, but the origin of life itself was based on the creative hand of God. This view takes both the natural operation of the universe and the activity of a transcendent creator seriously.

<u>Origins</u>

Based on a theistic point of view, the origin of life is from God Himself. Belief in a supernatural genesis is considered completely normal and obvious. As such, teaching about both natural laws and transcendent reality in our educational institutions is not problematic, as both are a part of the objectively real operation of reality.

Evolution/Variety of Life

When it comes to explaining the variety of life forms on earth, the supernatural is also the root of the explanation. As there is no true natural explanation for the wide variety of life forms that exist, it is not at all unnatural to posit God as the creator of all living things.

Theists do acknowledge the operation of evolutionary development as it pertains to physical life forms, but this relates only to micro-evolution, not macro-evolution as Naturalists would posit. Micro-evolution relates only to changes that occur in living things as they adapt to their environment. It in no way explains how the great variety of life forms on earth came into being.

Value of Life

Since Theists believe that mankind is a special creation of God, life itself takes on an objectively real purpose. Life is valuable because it is valuable to God.

The value of life is specifically tied to God's purposes. Since He created life purposefully, all life has value and should be cared for based on how He has revealed it to be meaningful. This may be expressed differently by the various theistic belief systems, but the general principle is true in all.

As such, the determination about whether or not taking a life is acceptable is based on God's revelation. He has determined the value of life and revealed to mankind how that should be expressed.

Typically, the life of human beings is deemed to be of highest value, though other forms of life are considered valuable, as well. The nature of that value is also expressed in God's revelation to mankind.

Law

The topic of law relates to the particular rules society uses to promote order within the culture. A theistic view of law is expressed in the principle of original intent. It is based on the idea that there exists an objective foundation for law that should not be violated. Law from this worldview perspective has an objective. In an ultimate sense, it is based on what God has revealed to be right and wrong. Using the principle of an ultimate, objective law, the idea of a constitutional-type document that forms the basis of all other laws has emerged. This approach looks to the foundational document as interpreted by its writers as its ultimate authority source.

As Theists believe in God, they look to Him to understand how the law should be expressed in order to create an orderly society. The result is a system of laws that do not change based merely on the whims of society or the personal preferences of those in power.

> *"As Theists believe in God, they look to Him to understand how the law should be expressed in order to create an orderly society."*

Politics

Politics involves the practice of administrating states or other political units. It is the management of a governmental system.

"Theistic politics ... draws its basic principles from God's revelation [and] the morality that informs the operation of government ... is based on His revelation."

Theistic politics is based on a governmental system that draws its basic principles from God's revelation. It is not that God necessarily establishes particular management practices, but the morality that informs the operation of the governmental system *is* based on His revelation. As such, politics is obliged to focus completely on accomplishing God's purposes in the world, based on His ways. Under some theistic systems, this may result in a theocracy of some type, but not necessarily: it all depends on the particular beliefs of individual theistic systems.

Regarding where the emphasis lies in relation to the people in the culture, this is also dependent upon the particular theistic system being dealt with. In some systems, the stress is on the legalistic interests of God. Systems based on this foundation tend not only to be theocratic, but it is the religious leaders who tend to direct the political organization. In other cases, the stress is on promoting the interests of the individual. In these cases, the priority of the individual is valued because of the high value God places on individual decisions. An example of a religious priority would be the political form found in nations governed by Islamic beliefs. An example of the priority of the individual would be the republican form of government found in the United States.

Economics

Economics is the study of the production, distribution, and

consumption of goods and services within a society. It also deals with the attempt to understand economic systems and how to manage them effectively. Theistic economics can branch off in different directions depending on the particular form of Theism being followed.

Some theistic belief systems lend themselves more to a command economy. These would be the ones that are legalistic and led by dictatorial leadership. Other theistic systems lean more toward a free enterprise approach. These are the ones that see human beings as God's stewards and put individual humans in a position to manage the material resources of society.

"Some ... theistic systems lean ... toward ... free enterprise [which sees] human beings as God's stewards and put individual humans in a position to manage the material resources of society."

History

History is the study of past events. Contained within this topic is an understanding of the purpose of human existence.

Theists understand history to be linear, in that it moves from past to present to future in a non-repetitive fashion. Based on theistic beliefs, history has meaning which emerges out of the purposes of God. Theists believe God created the material universe for a purpose, and that the progress of world societies is moving in history to accomplish His purpose.

Education

Education has two important components. First, it is the process of conveying specific knowledge and skills to others. Second, it involves imparting good judgment and wisdom. The goal is to pass the important elements of culture from generation to generation.

> "... God created the material universe for a purpose, and that the progress of world societies is moving in history to accomplish His purpose."

Education is a lifelong process; beginning at birth and continuing throughout life. It involves both formal and informal elements. Formal education is generally associated with participation in some kind of educational institution, while informal education is what people learn from other parts of life.

Theistic education is based on belief in God. Theists generally believe that the goal of education is to lead people to a greater understanding of God's will and ways. The ultimate purpose is that they may be able to express it more fully in the world.

> "... the goal of education is to lead people to a greater understanding of God's will and ways."

There are a couple of reasons Theists consider education to be important. First, there is true information every person needs to know in order to function effectively out in the world. By learning this information, individuals are able to be productive in the various places in life where they are serving God. It is also important because some of the knowledge people need to learn relates to how they express morality in daily life. It is considered that the application of this moral knowledge to daily situations is what creates a truly good life.

A Summary of Theism

As a worldview system, Theism believes that ultimate reality is found in God. God existed before the natural universe, and He created the material universe for a purpose. In order for human beings to know that purpose and live life based upon it, God revealed Himself and His ways to mankind. By understanding that revelation and living it out, humanity is able to please God and ultimately to spend eternity with Him in heaven.

> *"... Theism believes that ultimate reality is found in God."*

Discussion Questions

1. What is the most basic premise of a theistic worldview?
2. How do Theists answer the three essential worldview questions?
3. What would you expect various Theists to believe about Christianity and why?
4. Pick one of the following topics and explain it using a theistic understanding of reality: Theology, Philosophy, Anthropology, Sociology, Psychology, Communication, Ethics and Morality, Biology, Law, Politics, Economics, History, and Education.

Consider this ...

What would you think about someone who said the following things?

- God exists, and
- All of life is the result of naturalistic evolution and is not a creation of God, and
- I am a Christian, and
- I was Gandhi in a previous life, and
- Everyone goes to heaven when they die.

What would you say? Well, you should say that this person is really mixed up. Why? Because between these five statements there are numerous contradictions. It is impossible for them all to be true at the same time. A person can't hold Christian beliefs and atheistic beliefs at the same time. The same is true for Christian beliefs and pantheistic beliefs. A person who claims to be a Christian yet holds beliefs that do not fit in with the Christian faith cannot truly be a Christian.

That said, besides the many individuals who hold contradictory beliefs, there are many belief systems that do the same—some of them rather large and prominent.

Why should people be forced
to hold non-contradictory beliefs?

Chapter 8

A HYBRID WORLDVIEW
Wait! That's a contradiction.

In the strictest sense, the hybrid category is not a worldview at all. However, since there are many belief systems based on the hybrid concept, it is important to understand its existence and character. Hybrid belief systems take essential elements from two or more of the four worldview categories and attempt to merge them into one system.

But there is a huge problem with hybrids. Since every worldview literally contradicts every other worldview, all hybrids contain irreconcilable internal contradictions.

Believers in a hybrid system must ignore the contradictions in order to make sense of their beliefs in daily life. Interestingly, this is not typically a problem for most adherents. Humans are perfectly capable of compartmentalizing beliefs in ways that allow them to avoid even recognizing the contradictions. In fact, it is not unusual, at all, for adherents of virtually every belief system, including Christianity, to allow non-compatible beliefs into their personal lives.

"Hybrid belief systems take essential elements from two or more of the four worldview categories and attempt to merge them into one system."

Many of the more well-known hybrids in the

West tend to use Theism as a base, then combine elements of Naturalism or Far Eastern Thought. However, there are a huge number of other possibilities as well, so hybrids cannot be characterized precisely.

As such, it is impossible to quantify how hybrids, in a general sense, would deal with the various topics we have looked at in the previous chapters. Since every hybrid belief system has its own unique combination of beliefs, every one also has its own unique way of dealing with the various topics.

Some of the more prominent Hybrid belief systems include: New Age, Satanism, Unitarian Universalism, Scientology, Confucianism, Baha'I, Unification Church, and Christian Science.

Discussion Questions

1. What is the greatest problem hybrid belief systems face?
2. How do people manage to overcome the biggest problem facing hybrid belief systems?
3. What worldview category do hybrid belief systems fall into?
4. Of the hybrid systems listed above, which do you think is the most prominent? Which is the most accepted?

Consider this ...

Ask a person about the religious faith they follow, and they can generally, at least, give you a good overview. But, ask them to share their worldview beliefs and you are most likely to get a blank stare. Since every religious faith is established upon the foundation of a worldview system, you may wonder how that could be. The simple answer is that worldview beliefs are typically not acquired by learning about them intellectually. People get their worldview by living in an environment that is characterized by some particular set of beliefs, and they simply absorb them from their surroundings. Once thus learned, the result is that anything outside their perception simply seems unreal.

How did you acquire your worldview beliefs?

Chapter XI

How Do People Arrive at a Worldview
WERE YOU BORN WITH YOUR BELIEFS?

If a worldview is a set of assumptions, these assumptions must come from somewhere. So just how does a person come to a place in life where they personally affirm a particular set of beliefs?

In the grand scheme of things, there are three basic possibilities.
- The first one is the default, based on the fact that an individual is not aware of any other possibility.
- The second emerges as people become aware that other possibilities exist.
- The final one can occur when a person learns enough about worldviews that they are able to make a conscious decision to choose the one that seems right.

Let's take a look at the three possibilities now to see how this works.

Circumstances (Environment)

Think about the environment in which you grew up. As a child, it is quite unlikely that you were ever involved in discussions

---

"[The first possibility, and the default, is] an individual is not aware of any other possibilities."

---

about worldview. In fact, those who raised you were probably not even aware that more than one way of thinking about reality even existed. A worldview is a set of assumptions; and assumptions are generally not even consciously considered. So, you grew up around people who believed a certain way and lived life based on those beliefs.

Thinking a little more deeply, there is another factor that plays into the mix. Even if a family unit wanted to talk about worldview issues, a young child is not capable of understanding a topic of this complexity. Initially people's worldview emerges from the environment in which they were raised. When children are growing up, they don't have the perspective or the skills to analyze the things they are being taught. They simply live in a household and accept at face value the things they hear from the people who influence their lives.

A person's first beliefs are merely accepted based on the direct and indirect influences of the significant people in their lives. In fact, as a child, individuals do not even realize there are other perspectives than the ones they grew up hearing or otherwise experiencing. For many, this condition carries on throughout their entire lifetime. Even though there are multiple worldviews, unless a person is somehow brought to a conscious awareness of other belief possibilities, or they make a deliberate effort to discover them, all they will ever know are those they were exposed to when they were growing up. So a child grows up in a family environment and learns what is right and wrong, good and bad, based purely on what was considered acceptable in that environment

> *"Initially people's worldview emerges from the environment in which they were raised."*

(remember the sharp word, or hand slap, or even which way the toilet paper unrolled?). See? One way or another, you were learning your "worldview" all the time you were growing up.

Think back to the fish in the pond example in Chapter 4, when we were dealing with the worldview metaphors. Our fish lives in a set environment that contains certain plants, animals, and inanimate objects. If it could become aware of every single thing in and around its pond, it could be said to be a very intelligent fish. But regardless of how smart the fish might be and how much it knows about its environment, there are things it is totally unaware of. There are other ponds and other environments that contain other plants, animals, and objects that simply cannot be known by the fish.

A very young child's environment is much like that. Children learn the things associated with the people and places they grew up around and do not even realize that there are other possibilities. They only know what they know: what they learned seems right because they don't know there are even any other possibilities.

Crisis

It is not unusual, though, for individuals to be confronted, at some point in life, with different worldview beliefs. In fact, this often happens when a person is in high school or college— though the age at which this happens seems to be getting younger in many places. This can actually be a very traumatic event, as a person's worldview is believed at the most basic point of an individual's understanding of reality. It is, literally, the organizing principle for how they live life. So if one's understanding of reality gets upset, it turns the person's world upside down.

By way of personal example, while I never left my Christian faith, my college education brought me to the very edge. I was raised in a Christian home and was taught that the Bible was true. In high school, and later in college, I was taught naturalistic evolution in my biology classes. This directly contradicted the belief that I had learned growing up that God created life. Since I did not, at that time, understand anything about worldview beliefs, this created great internal conflict within my own mind. It took a lot of effort for me to work through this struggle. Personally, I was one that was not going to let go without a fight, and I did the study I needed to do to learn the truth about Naturalism. But I was being set up for a fall—by my education in school. Many of my friends succumbed.

The reason this kind of struggle occurs is that the combination of beliefs that a person holds at a worldview level creates mental, emotional, and spiritual stability in that individual's life. Also, as you will remember from our previous explanation, every worldview belief literally contradicts the worldview beliefs of every other worldview. So, when a conflict at this level occurs, it is a life-shaking experience.

> *"[If] one's understanding of reality gets upset, it turns the person's world upside down."*

Typically, when people encounter a different worldview, they are not prepared for it. As we saw in the last section, they don't even know there is the possibility that another way exists for looking at reality. Sure, they are aware of other beliefs, but are not aware that these other beliefs actually organize reality in a different way.

"[You may be] aware of other beliefs, but are not aware that these other beliefs actually organize reality in a different way."

So, when a challenge to their worldview emerges from a different set of worldview beliefs, it creates automatic conflict with one's own beliefs at the most fundamental level. If the conflicting beliefs come from a source that seems genuinely plausible, and if the individual encountering these strange beliefs does not have the foundational knowledge that allows him or her to critically evaluate these new beliefs, it will often create a belief crisis. With this new, plausible way of understanding reality coming forth, it causes a person to question their previous beliefs. And if this crisis is compelling enough, it is quite possible that the individual would even convert to another set of beliefs. Often when this happens, it results in a very dramatic and emotional experience.

I have had many interactions with people who tout the fact that they grew up in church and were baptized at a young age. But at some point in life, their Christian faith did not make sense to them anymore. It should be noted that the modern American educational system is actually built upon a non-Christian worldview—a naturalistic one to be precise. In the younger grades, kids are not necessarily taught that God does not exist, but they are taught "as if" He does not exist. Thus, when they get into high school and college, and are taught specifically that God does not exist, the worldview foundation is already in place so that Christian beliefs no longer sound plausible—but now—familiar naturalistic beliefs do. That is why we see so many high school kids—and especially college kids—leaving the faith in which they were raised.

Choice

There is a third way a person can come to own a worldview belief system—by choice. This way is the most difficult and least observed possibility. In this case, an individual has to make a deliberate effort to understand what is going on.

To be able to make a conscious choice, a person must have an understanding of more than one possibility. As we noted in the sections above, establishing one's worldview beliefs from the environment is not a conscious choice. In fact, the individual doesn't even realize there are other possibilities. Conversion by conflict is also not a conscious choice: it typically happens when a person's default belief, which they don't fully understand, is ambushed by a new belief they also do not understand.

To select a worldview based on a deliberate choice, an individual must come to actually understand the different worldview possibilities. At that point, they are in a position to choose the one that seems to correspond most closely with the way they perceive and live out their daily life.

I can honestly say, it is virtually impossible for a person to learn the various worldview possibilities based on sound bites. After all, we are dealing with what are primarily unconscious beliefs. This has to do with how people understand the way reality is organized. It certainly can be grasped by the average everyday person, but not without a significant amount of effort—

"[Selecting] a worldview [requires] actually understanding ... different worldview possibilities."

something that goes well beyond sound bites.

There are several reasons for this difficulty. First, without some background in this area, it is difficult to grasp the faith nature of worldview systems. Additionally, it is difficult to take new beliefs seriously, as they seem like they ought to be a fantasy. Finally, it is difficult to learn how to look through the lens of other worldview beliefs in order to understand "why" they don't correspond with reality. But this kind of understanding is what is required. To grasp the significance of worldview truly, a person must learn the possibilities, learn the strengths and weaknesses of the possibilities, and make an intelligent decision based on those possibilities. In fact, helping people do just that is one of the main reasons this book was written.

It might also be noted that making a decision about one's beliefs based on actually understanding the various alternatives tends to happen the least often of these three possibilities because most of us never put ourselves in a position to purposely become consciously aware of the existence of other worldview systems. We just don't know what we don't know. And without an awareness of the various possibilities—or that they even exist—individuals simply don't have the ability to compare the options.

Discussion Questions

1. What is the default worldview of every person on earth?
2. Why would a clash of worldviews cause some people to convert to a different belief?
3. What is necessary if a person is going to make a deliberate choice about what worldview belief to follow?

Consider this ...

When an Atheist asserts that the material universe is all that exists, how do they know that is true? When an Animist asserts there are many spirits, how do they know? When Far Eastern Thought believers assert that ultimate reality is impersonal, how do they know? When Theists say God exists, how do they know?

How do you know
that what you believe
... is true?

Chapter XII

Worldview Authority Sources
Is your Bible true?

"[The] four possible authority sources ... are: human reason, tradition, human experience, and revelation."

An authority source is the foundation upon which any given set of worldview beliefs is established. It is the most fundamental base for supporting the tenets of a belief system. As there are four basic worldview categories, there are four possible authority sources. These are: human reason, tradition, human experience, and revelation.

Every belief system is founded on one, or a combination, of these four.

The Four Authority Sources

Human Reason

Human Reason as an authority source is the use of individual reasoning to determine what is true and what is not true—what is right and what is wrong.

Human reason is the primary authority source for naturalistic belief systems. Naturalism is the belief that the only thing that exists is the natural universe. Naturalists believe there is no God and no transcendent reality. As such, everything that exists came into being based on the natural laws of the universe. Because of that, everything must ultimately be explainable using natural laws. Thus, Naturalists believe human beings can, in the end, come to understand and manipulate them, in an ultimate sense.

On account of their belief, Naturalists have no choice but to look to human reason as their ultimate authority source. After all, there is nothing else. The implications of this play out in every part of life. They believe that since all of reality can ultimately be explained using empirical science, the structuring of society must be done based on human reason.

Once again, they see no other possibility.

Tradition

Tradition as an authority source is the acceptance of beliefs and forms as truth that have been passed down from previous generations.

Tradition is the primary authority source of Animism.

While Animists believe in the existence of a transcendent reality, they also believe that it is symbiotically connected to the material world. That is, what happens in the material universe

"Naturalists have no choice but to look to human reason as their ultimate authority source."

directly affects what goes on in the spirit world, and vice versa. However, unlike Theists, Animists don't understand the spirits in the spirit world as beings that communicate personally to humans via propositional revelation (*i.e.,* using human language). As such, they must look to a different kind of authority source to understand what is right and wrong. That authority source is tradition.

Animists basically have to figure out morality by trial and error. The underlying assumption is that when humans perform actions that please the spirits, the spirits cause good things to happen to them. In the same way, when people act in ways that displease the spirits, bad things happen. Since there is no revelation by which the spirits actually communicate propositionally to humanity, people must carefully observe what is going on to try to discern what bad actions caused the bad results they see and what good actions caused the good results they see.

> *"Animists ... figure out morality by trial and error, [so they] make ... observations and draw ... cause-result relationships [which become] the tradition/authority source for their beliefs."*

Over time, as people make these observations and draw these cause-result relationships, they take note of them and pass the information down through the generations. This passed-down information, then, becomes the tradition which serves as the authority source for their beliefs.

Human Experience

Human Experience as an authority source is the attempt to determine truth based on a person's personal life experience.

Human experience is the authority source most closely associated with Far Eastern Thought—which is the belief that a transcendent reality does exist, but it is impersonal and immaterial. Since it is impersonal and immaterial, there is no conscious being in existence who can possibly reveal anything. And since ultimate reality, as it exists in the transcendent world, is immaterial, there is no kind of empirical methodology that can be used to get at it. The fact that it is impersonal *and* immaterial eliminates both revelation *and* human reason as possible ultimate authority sources.

Far Eastern Thought does depend on tradition to a certain extent to pass on its beliefs. But at a deeper level, it affirms that there is a means of direct interaction with transcendent reality. It teaches that, through various means, it is possible to experience the touch of the impersonal life force. This touch is not personal in the sense that propositional knowledge can be communicated. Nevertheless, it does allow individuals to "experience" the life force and intuitively come to understand how to accumulate good karma in order to progress toward escape from the suffering in

> *"Far Eastern Thought ... affirms ... direct interaction with ... the life force [to] intuitively ... understand how to accumulate good karma ..."*

the material world.

Revelation

The final authority source possibility is Revelation – an authority source in which the acceptance of information as truth is that the information is revealed from a transcendent source.

Revelation as an authority source is associated with theistic belief systems. Theism is the belief that a transcendent God exists, and that He is the creator and sustainer of the material universe. Thus, there is not only the belief that God exists, but that He resides outside the natural universe in a place that is not subject to the natural laws of the universe.

> *"God has crossed the barrier and revealed information about Himself and His ways to mankind."*

Since mankind is confined to the material universe, and God resides in a place that is outside it, human beings have no way to go to where God is in order to learn about Him. Thus, if God wants humans to know about Him and His ways, it is necessary that He take the initiative to reveal Himself. Thus, in every theistic belief system there is some authority source that assumes God has crossed the barrier and revealed information about Himself and His ways to mankind. Typically there is a holy book of some kind that is believed to contain that information. However, there are also other possibilities—such as a divine prophet that God uses as a spokesperson for Himself.

'Big Picture' Authority Sources

It is important to note that these four authority sources, as they relate to worldview beliefs, are in the 'big picture' category. Just as there are many belief systems within each worldview category, there are many possible specific authority sources also related to each category. For example, Christianity, Mormonism, and Islam are all theistic belief systems that look to revelation to support their beliefs. That said, each has its own specific revelation sources that it considers authoritative—Christianity recognizes the Bible; Mormonism recognizes the Book of Mormon, Doctrine and Covenants, The Pearl of Great Price, and the Bible (KJV); while Islam recognizes the Koran.

It is, of course, possible for any given belief system to acknowledge the existence of more than one big picture authority source. There will always be one, however, that is primary. The Christian faith, for example, acknowledges the validity of human reason, tradition, and human experience as secondary authority sources. That said, all of these secondary sources must be reconciled to its primary source of His revelation—the content of the Bible. In all cases, any secondary source must be subject to the primary one. Different primary and secondary authority sources, by necessity, lead to different beliefs.

'Small Picture' Authority Sources

As alluded to above, when addressing the topic of authority sources on a worldview level, we are not able to get at a specific, or 'small picture' source, only a 'big picture' category. At this level, an authority source is merely a point of reference—a given worldview must be based on, either: revelation, human reason, tradition, or human experience. We only get to precise, 'small picture' sources when we begin to discuss particular belief systems.

At the belief system level, it becomes possible to get very specific as to the actual source within the category. For instance:

- In the theistic worldview category, the primary, or 'big picture' authority source will always be some kind of revelation from God. However, until we know which theistic system we are dealing with, knowing which revelation to refer to is impossible. For instance, in Islam it would be the Koran, and in Christianity it is the Bible, *et al.*, as discussed.
- In Naturalism the 'big picture' authority source will always be human reason, but the direction of the reasoning will vary based on the particulars of the belief system with which you are dealing.
- In Animism the 'big picture' authority source will always be tradition, but the particular tradition reference will vary depending on the particular people group you are exploring.
- And in the same way, the 'big picture' authority source in Far Eastern Thought will always be human experience. Again, the way these beliefs are expressed will vary depending on the particular Far Eastern Thought belief system.

Discussion Questions

1. What are the four possible worldview authority sources and what distinguishes each one?
2. Why is it important to distinguish between big-picture and small-picture authority sources?

Consider this ...

Postmodernism is a naturalistic belief system that believes there is no such thing as objective truth. They believe that every person must define their own truth; that what is true for one person may not be true for another. This kind of belief, though, is absurd on its face. It is absurd because it uses an objective truth statement to assert that there is no such thing as objective truth. The statement, "<u>there is no such thing as objective truth</u>," is the assertion of an objective truth.

For something to actually be true, it must correspond with something that actually exists. And truth (reality) only exists in one form. Looking at a real-life example, if I believe that abortion is evil and someone else believes it is good, it is impossible for both of us to be right by any objective standard. Saying something is "right for me but not right for you" does not change the fact that these contradictory beliefs cannot both be "right" at the same time. The beliefs totally oppose one another. Just because I, or any other person, believes something does not make it true. And while we can certainly live life based on false beliefs "as if" they are true, that does not make them true.

Evaluating the "truth" of a worldview system must use evidence that goes beyond mere empirical inquiry. Of course, scientific study is also in the mix, but it is not enough by itself—necessary; but, not sufficient. The nature of worldview beliefs makes it impossible to prove them using the scientific method. That being the case, how, then, can anyone claim to know the truth?

Is it possible to know the truth?

Chapter XIII

Evaluating for the Truth of a Worldview
YOU DON'T GET TO MAKE UP YOUR OWN TRUTH.

At this point, we need to state again this basic premise overtly, that is: there is some way reality is actually structured, and it is not structured in any other way. Just because we may not know what that is, or that it cannot be demonstrated using experimental science, or that millions of people hold other beliefs, is completely beside the point. The fact is, there is some actual way reality is structured. Given that truth, there must be some way to get at it—and there is. At the same time, we must recognize that the evidence for it,

> *"[There] is some way reality is actually structured, and it is not structured in any other way."*

while it includes empirical evidence, is not limited to scientific proofs. The evidence must also include logic, deduction, and experiential confirmation

There is one other thing we need to be aware of, as well. Earlier we made a distinction between worldview beliefs and belief system beliefs. In this chapter, we are only dealing with worldview beliefs. Later we will take a further step and look at belief systems. While investigating, we also need to understand that it is possible for a generic worldview system to hold up while various belief systems within that worldview have contradictory beliefs in essential areas.

How Human Experience Matches with Worldview Doctrines

As we search for the truth about reality, one of the most important elements of our search relates to how the occurrences of life that people experience as they live day-to-day, match up with the tenets of a worldview system. As human beings, we live life in particular ways. Ideally, the way we live matches up with how reality is actually structured. If that is the case, our beliefs and experiences will align in ways that create harmony in our lives. If they do not line up, we will experience serious discord.

Human beings, though, have an interesting characteristic: we have the unique ability to disregard reality and live our lives based on beliefs that do not match up with how we actually experience life. In fact, there are millions of people who adhere to the different worldviews categorized as we have discussed. Since every worldview literally contradicts every other worldview, it is impossible for all of these to be right (that is, to correspond with actual reality). They could all be wrong, but it is only possible for one belief system to be right, as reality is structured in only one way. The fact that so many worldviews are held is a powerful confirmation of the human ability to ignore reality and live with inconsistent and contradictory beliefs. It also leads us to the conclusion that ...

> the majority of people on the planet, at any given time, live life "as if" what they believe about reality is true, when, in fact, it is not.

Why Doctrine and Human Experience Must Match Up

[Please note: The use of "human experience" here is not a reference to it as an authority source (as we used it earlier) but rather to the actual occurrences of life that people experience as they live day to day.]

The way the beliefs of a worldview system match up with the day-to-day human experiences of lived-lives is a critical element in getting at the truth or falsity of any particular belief system. If there isn't a match, it means either that the system is wrong, or that our human experience is wrong.

- If human experience is wrong, we can't reliably make judgments about anything. Since we experience what we experience, if what we experience is wrong, we wouldn't even know it.
- If the belief system is wrong, the only way to correct the problem is to discover the truth and change the beliefs to align to the truth.

On the other hand, if a person's human experience does match up with the doctrines of a particular worldview system, it is quite strong evidence that an individual is moving in the right direction. Again, we are not talking exclusively about empirical proof because getting at the truth or falsity of a worldview using only empirical methods is impossible. Rather, we are dealing with specific types of evidence that can be applied to our search.

In examining the four worldview systems above, the only one that completely matches with human experience is Theism. As such, we have powerful, positive evidence that the ultimate

---

"One of the strongest lines of evidence regarding the truth or falsity of a worldview system relates to how it matches up with the way human beings experience life."

---

truth about the nature of reality lies within that system. That being said, there are numerous, and contradictory, belief systems even within Theism. In the end, it becomes necessary to delve beyond the worldview level to discover ultimate truth. Still, finding the worldview system that corresponds to the way reality is actually structured is a necessary starting point. (Note: Ultimately, only one belief system—which is associated with one particular worldview—can represent actual reality. The Christian faith is that one belief system).

One of the strongest lines of evidence regarding the truth or falsity of a worldview system relates to how it matches up with the way human beings experience life. By comparing areas generally acknowledged to be the important parts of human existence with the presuppositions of each worldview, we can see how they match up.

Before we begin making those comparisons, though, we need to identify first the things everyone would agree are true reflections of human experience. We-will use these nine:

1. *We experience life as personal, self-aware beings.* As humans, we possess the characteristics of personhood and are aware of our own existence.

2. *We have a sense of transcendence.* Most human beings acknowledge a sense that something exists beyond the material universe. (This does not mean that everyone acknowledges an actual transcendent existence, only that there is a sense of it.) This has been true across cultures and time in every part of the world.

3. *We experience life in relationships.* Humans have a need for relationship that goes beyond mere biological necessity. This need is seen in the desire we have for non-sexual interactions, as well as in selfless acts toward others.

4.   We experience life based in spiritual qualities. There are human-only qualities that go beyond mechanistic, biological function. These include such characteristics as creativity, self-consciousness, self-determination, and the like.

5.   We experience life based on natural laws. It is apparent that the operation of the material universe is based on natural laws. It is possible for human beings to work with natural laws to create benefit for themselves. On the other side, it is impossible to manipulate the material universe in ways that run counter to these laws.

6.   We are capable of knowledge. Human beings have a unique ability to acquire, hold, and self-consciously use knowledge.

7.   We have a sense of morality. All humans live life based on some system of morality. Various people may define this differently or disregard what they believe to be right. Nevertheless, the moral sense is operative regardless.

8.   We experience time as linear. Human beings experience time as a non-repetitive sequence of events that moves from past to present to future.

9.   We experience the world as objective. Every human being lives life as if the world exists as an objective reality. Despite any philosophical attempt to define it in another way, all must live "as if" it is true.

In the next few chapters, we will look at the doctrines of the four worldview belief categories and compare them with way human beings actually experience life in order to see how they match up. Places where they match are evidence of the truth of a worldview system. Places where they don't match become evidence that there are serious problems with the worldview.

Discussion Questions

1. Why is it important for human experience and an individual's beliefs to match up?
2. What happens when human experience and individual beliefs don't match up?

Consider this ...

I have had numerous discussions with Atheists who insist that I prove that the Christian faith is true using naturalistic presuppositions. That is, they want me to prove that God exists based on some kind of experimental science. When I try to explain to them that it is impossible, they generally double down and chastise me for not doing it. Then, when I point out they can't even do that with their own worldview beliefs, the general reaction is disbelief. They really do believe that their point of view not only can be proven by science, but has been. It generally comes as a great shock when they finally realize they can't prove their worldview beliefs by science — that it is, essentially, a religious position.

What would a Naturalist have to do to prove Naturalism is true?

Chapter XIV

Evaluating the Truth of Naturalism
How do you know you came from apes?

Naturalism is a mixed bag when it comes to the alignment of human experience and naturalistic doctrine. Some things match up, while others don't. The places where doctrine and experience don't match provide strong indications of serious problems within the naturalistic worldview. Let's explore the nine human experiences and see how they match up with the worldview beliefs of Naturalism.

1. We experience life as personal, self-aware beings.

There are two primary approaches Naturalists tend to take regarding an understanding of the human person. Both of these approaches rely strictly on Darwinistic evolution to explain their belief.

The first naturalistic approach is determinism. Since in naturalistic thought, humans are understood to be nothing more than highly evolved animal creatures, our perceived ability to be self-aware must actually be an illusion. Based on a naturalistic

---

"The places where doctrine and experience don't match provide strong indications of serious problems within the naturalistic worldview."

---

paradigm, the entirety of the operation of the physical body can be accounted for based purely on biological function. The perception that people have that they are personal, self-aware beings can really be nothing more than chemical and electrical reactions within a brain that has evolved highly enough to allow us to operate "as if" we are self-aware beings, when, in fact, that cannot be the case.

The other naturalistic approach actually affirms that human creatures are self-aware beings. Based on this paradigm, our brains have evolved to a high enough level to make it possible for that kind of self-awareness to actually exist. Those using this approach will acknowledge that while they don't understand how this could be, they are confident that when science advances far enough, it will become evident.

The big problem with these two approaches, however, is that they are both faith assumptions. There is no scientific evidence available to show that either of these beliefs could possibly be true. While Naturalists live life "as if" they are personal, self-aware beings, their doctrine has no way to explain how this might be true.

2. We have a sense of transcendence.

Naturalists may acknowledge that human beings have a "sense" of transcendence, but they assert that this sense is actually nothing more than feelings. The thought is that the human species evolved a natural cognitive sense as a survival mechanism; this sense gives humans a feeling that there is something beyond themselves. The assertion is, however, that since there is nothing transcendent to the material universe, this sense does not reflect reality. Belief in anything supernatural is dismissed out of hand. As for how Naturalism backs up this claim, it must resort to simply making unverified and unverifiable assumptions. The truth is, there is no science to back up this evolutionary claim.

3. We experience life in relationships.

In naturalistic doctrine, relationships are acknowledged to exist. That said, they are seen only as biological necessities (to continue the species), rather than corresponding to any objectively real spiritual connection between individuals. As noted above, all of life, including human life, is assumed to exist based purely on naturalistic processes. Since Naturalists believe that humans are not, in fact, personal, self-aware creatures, the ability to self-consciously develop relationships cannot be an actual reality. They believe that human beings only "seem" to be able to develop them. This is another place where Naturalists have no choice but to live life "as if" personal relationships are actually self-conscious, self-determined realities, but their doctrine can't support it. There is no scientific basis for this kind of doctrinal claim. It is based strictly on the philosophical presupposition that material reality is all that exists.

4. We experience life based in spiritual qualities.

"Spiritual qualities," as defined in the previous chapter, are acknowledged by Naturalists to exist. However, based on naturalistic beliefs, these qualities can only be physiological elements; which became a part of the makeup of the human species based on natural evolutionary development. As before, though, Naturalists are unable to point to any scientific proof to defend this belief. They assert it purely because natural processes are all that they acknowledge to exist. Rather than this being a scientific conclusion, it is based purely on philosophical presuppositions.

5. We experience life based on natural laws.

The operation of natural laws is one of the places where naturalistic doctrine actually does align with human experience. In fact, it is a central element of a naturalistic belief system. Naturalists affirm, as one of the cornerstones of the worldview, that natural laws are able to explain all of reality. This belief is considered absolute and is based on human observation of the universe in action. Regardless of this belief, there is no empirical basis for positively affirming that the natural universe is all that exists.

6. We are capable of knowledge.

In naturalistic belief, human knowledge is recognized to exist. In fact, an explanation of the operation of reality is dependent upon the existence of actual knowledge. However, the human capacity to acquire, hold, and use knowledge is seen as nothing more than the physiological ability to store and retrieve information using a sophisticated biological computer (the human brain). As previously discussed, the self-conscious use of knowledge requires an objectively real self-consciousness to exist—which cannot be shown based on naturalistic presuppositions. In Naturalism, knowledge can only be the functioning of a highly evolved brain. Again, there is no scientific justification for this belief. It is based strictly on the philosophical presupposition that no supernatural reality exists.

7. We have a sense of morality.

For Naturalists, a sense of right and wrong is, typically, acknowledged to exist. In fact, in real life, Naturalists live "as if" there is such a thing as moral right and wrong—though it is considered to be based on a relative foundation rather than some objective standard. For Naturalists, morality is nothing more than an evolutionary development; which has as its only possible purpose to promote the survival of the species.

Since Naturalists acknowledge no such thing as a transcendent reality, there is no place beyond the material universe from which a moral code or system could emerge. The only possibility they acknowledge is that human beings make up their own moral codes based on the felt needs of individuals and groups. Beyond that, they believe that human beings must enforce morality by coercion. This belief about morality is based solely on the philosophical presupposition that the natural universe is all that exists. There is no scientific basis for this assertion. In spite of that, all Naturalists live life "as if" objective morality exists at some level.

8. We experience time as linear.

As time is one of the essential elements of physical reality, Naturalism wholeheartedly embraces humanity's experience of time as moving from past to present to future. In fact, this is another of the cornerstones of a naturalistic worldview. This must be so because, to Naturalists, the physical universe is considered to be the ultimate form of reality. This belief is asserted due to human observation of the universe in action, and is based on the philosophical presupposition that the natural universe is all that exists.

9. We experience the world as objective.

The naturalistic understanding that the material universe is an objective reality is another place where naturalistic belief matches up with human experience. In fact, the concept of an objective world is embraced as one of the cornerstones of Naturalism; as the physical universe is considered to be the ultimate form of reality. There is no means, based on naturalistic belief, to explain how the natural universe came to exist as an objective reality, although it does acknowledge its objective existence.

As we compare the beliefs of a naturalistic worldview to the way human beings experience life, we see that there are a few places where naturalistic beliefs and human experience matches up. That said, even in those places, Naturalism is unable to account for why or how it could possibly be so. Table 14-1 captures these conclusions.

TABLE 14-1. EVALUATION: THE TRUTH OF NATURALISM

HUMAN EXPERIENCE	NATURALIST'S EXPERIENCE	DO THEY MATCH?
Personal, self-aware beings	YES	NO
Sense of transcendence	YES	NO
Life in relationships	YES	NO
Spiritual Qualities	YES	NO
Life based on Natural Laws	YES	YES
Capable of Knowledge	YES	NO
Sense of Morality	YES	NO
Experience Time as Linear	YES	YES
Experience the World as Objective	YES	YES

"In spite of the fact that Naturalism asserts that all of reality can be accounted for based on empirical proofs, it is unable to use empiricism to account for its beliefs."

In spite of the fact that Naturalism asserts that all of reality can be accounted for based on empirical proofs, it is unable to use empiricism to account for its beliefs. The fact is, Naturalism is a faith system. And the only reason Naturalists can give for believing naturalistic assumptions is that they have faith in their naturalistic presuppositions.

Discussion Questions

1. In what ways does naturalistic belief match up with human experience?
2. In what ways does naturalistic belief not match up with human experience?
3. What does the fact that there are places where naturalistic belief does and does not match up with human experience tell you about the viability of Naturalism?

Consider this ...

As I have interacted with various people who self-identify as Animists, what I have found is that very few who live in a non-animistic culture are truly Animists. It is fascinating how certain people like to latch onto exotic beliefs or ideas. It is as if they are looking for new ways to be noticed, rather than actually embracing an actual belief.

Most of the Animists I have talked to assert certain animistic beliefs, but they also tend to inject non-Animistic beliefs into the mix. It is not unusual for them to claim, for instance, that Animism preceded monotheism, then use naturalistic evolutionary theory to justify their contention. It is also not unusual for many of them to mix in a little Far Eastern Thought ideology for good measure.

What would an Animist have to do to prove that Animism is true?

Chapter XV

Evaluating the Truth of Animism
How do you know your animal spirit not a demon?

The Animistic worldview is also a mixed bag when it comes to aligning human experience to its worldview doctrine. The problems with Animism, though, are framed differently than what we saw in Naturalism. As we will see, Animism does have some beliefs that correspond to human experience. But as we will also see, there are important issues that cannot be resolved.

1. We experience life as personal, self-aware beings.

Animistic belief assumes that humans are personal self-aware beings, but can point to no particular reason why this is true. The animistic basis for making this assertion comes simply by observing how individual humans live daily life. The biggest problem this position faces is that there is nothing they can

> *"Animism does have some beliefs that correspond to human experience. But ... there are important issues that cannot be resolved."*

point to as an authority for making this claim. Animism does not use scientific evidence, nor does it look to revealed evidence to support its position. So while the doctrine matches with human experience in many areas, there is no support for it other than tradition and subjective human experience—which is not necessarily reliable. It is possible to interpret experiences in different ways.

2. *We have a sense of transcendence.*

A sense of transcendence is also a core component of Animism; and, as with the belief above, is assumed to be true based primarily on human experience. Animists express this belief by showing respect for and homage to the spirits and gods they recognize. The problem that exists, however, is that there is no basis for acknowledging any particular spiritual beings. In fact, different animistic groups recognize entirely different spirit beings. A simple feeling that a transcendent reality exists does not provide any material or immaterial justification that it actually exists.

3. *We experience life in relationships.*

The fact of the existence of actual, self-conscious human relationships is assumed in animistic belief. As with the previous elements, though, Animism provides no reason for the existence of these relationships, as there is no philosophical basis for their existence. It is acknowledged simply because it is the default observable situation in human society. As such, animistic doctrine struggles to explain why it matches up with human experience, since there is no discernible reason why these relationships exist.

4. *We experience life based in spiritual qualities.*

While human beings naturally express spiritual qualities in the mundane, day-to-day experiences of life, these qualities are not acknowledged, or expressed, in ways that allow animistic cultures to move beyond primitive life circumstances. For instance, whenever there is a problem or issue that needs to be solved, the solution is understood to be related to appeasing offended spirits rather than by using human spiritual qualities to find answers. As such, the spiritual qualities, which are innate in humanity, are minimized and not fully acknowledged.

5. We experience life based on natural laws.

Animists certainly must live their daily lives according to the operation of natural laws; it is impossible to do otherwise. That said, their embrace of natural laws is mitigated by the belief that spirits also engage the physical world and influence what happens. While Animists must live "as if" the world operates by natural laws, they don't always acknowledge that fact. One part of animistic belief also assigns supernatural causation to things that happen in daily life—some of which are actually explainable by science.

Based on an animistic point of view, there is no objective reason to assign causality to either the natural or supernatural. The determination is made based strictly on whether or not they are able to intellectually understand the cause. Thus, their understanding of reality is skewed by not being able to effectively distinguish between the natural and the supernatural.

6. We are capable of knowledge.

Animists assume that human beings are capable of knowledge as it relates to the routine elements of life. This is, once again, based on simple observation of how humans operate out in the world. That said, things that lie beyond their limited knowledge are automatically attributed to supernatural causes. As such, Animists do not tend to seek natural answers for anything they do not already understand. This lack of ability to distinguish between the natural and the supernatural is problematic, because it is that ability that allows one to differentiate between fantasy and reality. In this area, animistic belief does not match up well to human experience.

7. We have a sense of morality.

To Animists, human morality is considered to be an integral part of the way the universe operates. In Animistic thought, moral judgments are based on a belief that what humans do in the material world affects the spirits in the spirit world. As such, human actions that create problems in the spirit world are immoral, and those that promote harmony in the spirit world are moral. The way humans ultimately discern the difference is by observing their own world. When bad things begin happening for individuals or the clan, it can be assumed that some bad (immoral) act has occurred and must be corrected. When things are going well, there is peace and prosperity, which indicates people are living out a proper morality. Over generations, as this is observed, an understanding of morality is developed based on the observations.

The problem is, as with some of the previous categories, there is nothing beyond human experience and tradition to base their beliefs upon. No individual or group is able to objectively justify any particular understanding of moral right and wrong, or their reasons for following it.

8. We experience time as linear.

Animists assume a linear understanding of time, as this seems to be the natural default of human experience. They recognize time as moving from past to present to future. That being said,

"The greatest problem animistic belief has matching up to human experience lies in its lack of ability to provide reasons for its beliefs."

this is another place where animistic belief seems to match up with human experience, but where there is no philosophical justification for it.

Because of the lack of justification for this position, the sense of correspondence with human experience is problematic.

9. We experience the world as objective.

The experience of the world as objective is another place where the animistic viewpoint essentially matches up with human experience, but the justification for it is problematic. Animists embrace belief in an objective world because of their observation of the universe in action. At the same time, the spirit world is acknowledged as an objective reality that intrudes into the physical world in particular ways. The problem is, there is no means of affirming nor justifying the way this interaction takes place, other than by their philosophical presuppositions.

The greatest problem animistic belief has matching up to human experience lies in its lack of ability to provide reasons for its beliefs. Animists observe what exists and how things seem to work in the everyday world, but they also interject transcendent notions into the mix without having any justification for doing so. They don't begin with their observation of the world. Rather, they begin with their animistic presuppositions, then fit their observations into that as best they can. The lack of reasons for their beliefs create serious doubts as to the degree human experience and animistic belief match up. Table 15-1 captures these conclusions.

TABLE 15-1. EVALUATION: THE TRUTH OF ANIMISM

HUMAN EXPERIENCE	ANIMIST'S EXPERIENCE	DO THEY MATCH?
Personal, self-aware beings	YES	YES
Sense of transcendence	YES	YES
Life in relationships	YES	YES
Spiritual Qualities	YES	PARTIALLY
Life based on Natural Laws	YES	PARTIALLY
Capable of Knowledge	YES	PARTIALLY
Sense of Morality	YES	YES
Experience Time as Linear	YES	YES
Experience the World as Objective	YES	PARTIALLY

Discussion Questions

1. In what ways does animistic belief match up with human experience?
2. In what ways does animistic belief not match up with human experience?
3. What does the fact that there are places where animistic belief does and does not match up with human experience tell you about the viability of Animism?

Consider this ...

I once had a conversation with an adherent of Christian Science: this is a belief system that claims to be Christian, but is based on Far Eastern Thought. In this conversation the other person wrote me and objected to how I characterized Christian Science as pantheistic rather than Christian. In my replies to him, I carefully differentiated and contrasted the beliefs of biblical Christianity to those of Christian Science. I showed him how it was impossible for them to both be true.

In spite of our very clear and sharp differences about what we believed, the discussion was actually very polite. In the end, I expressed the following thoughts:

> If your belief truly reflects reality, I don't know where that leaves me. But if *my* understanding is true, you are separated from God—regardless of your feelings or belief. I, too, will conclude with a wish that you will find salvation in Jesus Christ—the king of Kings and lord of Lords.

In his next, and final, reply, he wrote the most amazing thing. He said, "Nice that we conclude on the same note. I'll take that as a sign of how He truly is king of Kings and lord of Lord(s)."

In spite of the fact that our beliefs could not be further apart, because of his Far Eastern Thought belief foundation, he still saw our basic beliefs as being on par with each other. Simply amazing!

What would a Far Eastern Thought-believer have to do to prove that Far Eastern Thought is true?

Chapter XVI

Evaluating the Truth of Far Eastern Thought
FORCE? WHAT FORCE?

O f all the worldview possibilities, Far Eastern Thought is the worldview system that is most difficult to reconcile with human experience. Because of its foundational structure, Far Eastern Thought essentially dismisses human experience altogether as a means of seeking to understand reality. It does this by affirming that what we experience in the material universe does not reflect reality at all. This belief asserts that transcendent reality is impersonal and immaterial, and everything we experience as a part of this reality is illusory.

1. We experience life as personal, self-aware beings.

Those who follow a Far Eastern Thought worldview live life "as if" human beings are personal, self-aware creatures. Anyone who lives in the material universe has no choice but to do so. At the same time, they assert that this point of view is an illusion. This is not to say they deny the existence of the natural universe. Rather, they believe that, in an ultimate sense, every element of reality that they experience as personal, is actually impersonal. As such, this sense of self-awareness and personality must be an illusion.

> *"Far Eastern Thought ... [affirms] that what we experience in the material universe does not reflect reality at all."*

2. We have a sense of transcendence.

Far Eastern Thought teaches that an actual transcendent reality does exist; however, they also teach that this existence is strictly impersonal. The problem human beings have with this is that any experience we might have of transcendence in this life must somehow be experienced through our senses as a "personal" experience. This completely contradicts Far Eastern Thought doctrine. Since reality is understood to be strictly impersonal, human beings must also be, in an ultimate sense, impersonal. Human self-awareness of this sense, then, must be an illusion. At that point, the question becomes, "How can one know that there even is a transcendent existence if personality is not a part of ultimate reality?" This dilemma is impossible to reconcile.

3. We experience life in relationships.

Since relationships can only exist in a reality where personal beingness exists, and since Far Eastern Thought asserts that personality does not reflect ultimate reality, the idea of personal human relationships is, in the end, meaningless. It, too, is an illusion. Once again, though, humans who live in the material universe have no choice but to live "as if" relationships are important. Interestingly, Far Eastern Thought actually requires the operation of relationships for the purpose of creating bodies into which the impersonal life force can reincarnate. There is no objective evidence to back up the Far Eastern Thought point of view in this regard. And even if there were, it would have to be dismissed as illusory.

4. We experience life based in spiritual qualities.

When it comes to spiritual qualities, Far Eastern Thought, once again, run into a problem related to personality. Human beings experience spiritual qualities in a personal manner as a part of their human existence. Doctrinally, though, Far Eastern Thought believers assert that ultimate reality is impersonal. Since the life force is impersonal in an absolute sense, and spiritual qualities are essentially personal, these qualities must also be understood to be an illusion. Again, human experience and Far Eastern Thought doctrine are at opposite ends of the spectrum.

5. *We experience life based on natural laws.*

Far Eastern Thought asserts that ultimate reality is a transcendent, impersonal life force, and that the material universe is not a true expression of that reality. As such, the natural laws that operate within the material universe are also illusory. We are, once again, in a place where human experience and Far Eastern Thought doctrine contradict one another.

6. *We are capable of knowledge.*

Human beings certainly live life as if knowledge exists, but we again run into the same problem as before: human knowledge is an expression of personality. And since ultimate reality is understood to be impersonal, we are again faced with a human characteristic that does not mesh with Far Eastern Thought doctrine. Far Eastern Thought considers human knowledge ultimately to be illusory. Thus, what human beings seem to know is not characteristic of the way they believe reality actually exists.

7. *We have a sense of morality.*

As we consider the concept of morality, we are again interacting with something that is an expression of personality. Since ultimate reality is understood to be impersonal, morality must also be considered an illusion. This creates a problem because in Far Eastern Thought doctrine, right and wrong do exist as a function of karma. However, in the ultimate sense, there can be no right and wrong because awareness of it would be a personal observation. Far Eastern Thought doctrine understands the cosmos to be perpetually in a state of perfection, with karma continually balancing everything out. Additionally, Far Eastern Thought adherents assert a form of morality that defines how good and bad karma is expressed. This is another contradiction that cannot be reconciled.

8. We experience time as linear.

Far Eastern Thought live daily life "as if" the existence of past, present, and future are a reality. However, Far Eastern Thought doctrine asserts that reality actually exists in a state of eternity; operating cyclically. Since time is a function of material reality, and is experienced in a linear fashion, it too is understood to be an illusion. Here we have another place where human experience and Far Eastern Thought doctrine contradict one another.

"Interestingly, there are, literally, no places where Far Eastern Thought presuppositions match up with human experience."

---

9. We experience the world as objective.

Even though Far Eastern Thought believers live in the world "as if" it is an objective reality, its doctrine asserts that material reality is an illusion. Ultimate reality is understood to be immaterial. Since the material does not reflect the truth about impersonal reality, it cannot be a true expression of ultimate reality.

Interestingly, there are, literally, no places where Far Eastern Thought presuppositions match up with human experience. All human experience is based on some kind of expression of personality and materiality—which Far Eastern Thought denies is real. The fact that Far Eastern Thought doctrine does not match up at all with human experience is very strong evidence that there is something wrong with the Far Eastern Thought worldview itself. Table 16-1 captures these conclusions.

TABLE 16-1. EVALUATION: THE TRUTH OF FAR-EASTERN THOUGHT (FET)

HUMAN EXPERIENCE	FET EXPERIENCE	DO THEY MATCH?
Personal, self-aware beings	YES	NO
Sense of transcendence	YES	NO
Life in relationships	YES	NO
Spiritual Qualities	YES	NO
Life based on Natural Laws	YES	NO
Capable of Knowledge	YES	NO
Sense of Morality	YES	NO
Experience Time as Linear	YES	NO
Experience the World as Objective	YES	NO

Discussion Questions

1. In what ways does Far Eastern Thought belief match up with human experience?
2. In what ways does Far Eastern Thought belief not match up with human experience?
3. What does the fact that there are no places where Far Eastern Thought belief matches up with human experience tell you about the viability of Far Eastern Thought?

Consider this ...

There are people who get confused when dealing with Theism. For instance, since Christianity, Islam, Mormonism, and Jehovah's Witnesses all have such different beliefs, many wonder how they could possibly all fit into the same worldview category.

The answer is really not that complicated: it is absolutely possible for many different faith systems to assert belief in the existence of God, yet disagree about who God is or what He is like. It is possible for different beliefs to agree that human beings are spiritual creatures that live in a physical body, yet have very different beliefs as to the nature of the human person. It is not a strange thing at all for various belief systems to assert that pleasing God will get a person to heaven, yet disagree about what it means to please God.

Theism is a big picture category. Just because many different belief systems all fall into the same worldview category, and believe in the same overall structure of reality, it does not necessarily follow that they all understand the specifics of that reality in the same way.

What would a Theist have to do to prove that Theism is true?

Chapter XVII

Evaluating the Truth of Theism
HOW DO YOU KNOW THAT YOUR GOD IS THE TRUE GOD?

In a big picture sense, Theism represents the way reality is actually structured. It acknowledges both a spiritual realm, which exists outside the material universe, and a physical universe, which operates by natural laws. This does not mean that every theistic belief system represents the way reality is actually structured. There is a particular way reality is structured and it is not structured in any other way. The fact that each theistic system proposes a different God with different character traits and different systems of morality, makes plain the fact that not every theistic belief system is true. Still, when working only on a worldview level, we can assert that the theistic approach is the correct one. It best matches up with the way human beings experience reality.

"In a big picture sense, Theism ... acknowledges both a spiritual realm, which exists outside the material universe, and a physical universe, which operates by natural laws."

---

1. We experience life as personal, self-aware beings.

In all Theistic belief systems, God is revealed to be a person who created mankind with personal, self-aware characteristics.

This matches with how human beings experience the human condition.

2. *We have a sense of transcendence.*

Theism sees God as a transcendent person based on His revelation of Himself to mankind. Human beings are understood to be creatures that were created with the ability to recognize God's existence. Human experience across time and cultures acknowledges this kind of understanding about God by human beings, and this is one line of evidence that transcendent reality actually exists.

3. *We experience life in relationships.*

The particulars of the way relationships are understood to operate vary, based on the specific form of Theism being dealt with. Almost without exception, theistic belief systems affirm a God who operates in some kind of relationship with mankind. They also affirm that the human person was created to live in relationships with other human beings, and it sanctions various societal institutions in support of these relationships. Once again, theistic beliefs match up with the way human beings experience reality.

4. *We experience life based in spiritual qualities.*

In theistic systems, God is revealed to be a spiritual being who made mankind as a material creature with the spiritual qualities humans exhibit. This matches up with the way human beings experience their own personhood.

5. *We experience life based on natural laws.*

Theistic beliefs affirm that material reality is based on a fixed set of natural laws, while also acknowledging that God exists outside of that reality. It goes on to assert that He has the ability to intervene in His creation without upsetting the operation of those laws. This matches up nicely with the way human beings experience life on earth.

6. We are capable of knowledge.

Theism asserts that God created mankind with the ability to possess knowledge. This matches up with the way human beings experience material life.

7. We have a sense of morality.

In Theism, God is revealed to be a being with a particular character; and it is His character that defines the boundaries of morality. This morality is shared with mankind through revelation. The specifics of the revelation will vary based on the particulars of a given theistic system; but it is not the differences in moral beliefs that are important as much as the belief in the viability of a revelation.

As an extension of that, in Theism, human beings are understood to have a sense of that morality as an innate part of their being. This also matches up with the way human beings experience life.

8. We experience time as linear.

In theistic belief systems, God is typically revealed to have established the material universe as a time-based reality that moves from past to present to future. This is, certainly, how human beings experience time.

9. We experience the world as objective.

Theism asserts that God is an actual objective person who created an objectively real material universe. Our human experience affirms the objectivity of the world we live in.

As we look at the basic doctrines of Theism and compare them to the way human beings experience real life, it is easy to see that theistic presuppositions match up very closely with human experience. Table 17-1 captures these conclusions.

TABLE 17-1. EVALUATION: THE TRUTH OF THEISM

HUMAN EXPERIENCE	THEIST'S EXPERIENCE	DO THEY MATCH?
Personal, self-aware beings	YES	YES
Sense of transcendence	YES	YES
Life in relationships	YES	YES
Spiritual Qualities	YES	YES
Life based on Natural Laws	YES	YES
Capable of Knowledge	YES	YES
Sense of Morality	YES	YES
Experience Time as Linear	YES	YES
Experience the World as Objective	YES	YES

"[That] theistic presuppositions match up very closely with human experience ... is positive evidence that [Theism] is the one that reflects the actual structure of reality."

This agreement is positive evidence that a theistic worldview is the one that reflects the actual structure of reality.

Discussion Questions

1. In what ways does theistic belief match up with human experience?
2. In what ways does theistic belief not match up with human experience?
3. What does the fact that theistic beliefs match up with human experience at every point tell you about the viability of Theism?

Consider this ...

"How do you know that Christianity is true, and that the God of the Bible is the true God?" This is a question I get a lot. Interestingly, the people who ask it the most are Atheists who don't want to believe it. To acknowledge that truth would require that they become accountable to Him. In order to avoid this, they require that I prove his existence using a naturalistic formula. They want me to, somehow, do some kind of scientific experiment to demonstrate God is real.

The crazy thing is, they can't even show that their own belief is true using their own worldview beliefs. Based on that fact, it seems rather absurd to put that requirement on me when my beliefs don't even fit into that category.

Belief in God, based on biblical Christianity, is personal. God is a real person and he has revealed himself to us in personal terms. There is some empirical evidence we can bring to the table, as well as logic, deduction, human experience, and tradition. But the ultimate revelation God has made is personal. The faith of a believer in Christ is confirmed because we know him.

What is the ultimate proof that God exists?

Chapter XVIII

The Structure of Truth—Biblical Christianity
A CHRISTIAN WORLDVIEW IS MORE THAN DOCTRINE.

After identifying Theism as the worldview system that represents the way reality is actually structured, we must still deal with the fact that there are numerous theistic belief systems that contradict one another. This means that even after we know the truth about worldview systems, we still have to investigate further to determine which belief system within Theism represents the truth.

It is beyond the scope of this book to go all in on that particular investigation. However, at the very least, we can identify the

> *"Any belief system that is not the truth is going to have problems that cannot be overcome."*

problems that must be resolved in that investigation. Any belief system that is not the truth is going to have problems that cannot be overcome. Those problems fall into a couple of different categories.

One category relates to problems with historical accuracy. As you examine the history of any false belief system, you will come across problems where actual history does not match up with what is taught in the belief system. Some examples of this can be seen in Mormonism regarding the claims of Joseph Smith; that some of the revelation he received from God was written in reformed Egyptian hieroglyphics, the claim that certain Pacific Islanders were descended from the ancient Hebrews, and other disprovable contentions.

Another category relates to problems of consistency within the belief system itself. As you examine the teachings of false belief systems, you will inevitably find internal contradictions. An example of this can be found in Islam; where they have had to resort to claiming certain revelations supersede previous ones because the newer ones literally contradict the older.

The actual truth, though, will not have these kinds of problems. It will be fully consistent and historically accurate. It is only the Christian faith that passes all of the tests. This does not mean that one can empirically prove the Christian faith to be true, since it is impossible to prove empirically that any worldview belief is true. It also doesn't mean that it is possible to definitively explain every question that can be imagined. But it does mean that the available evidence all points to the truth of the Christian faith. This also aligns nicely with our personal experience of entering into a personal relationship with God through Jesus Christ.

If the Christian faith is the ultimate expression of truth, it is important for us to have a sense of what the faith looks like. To get at this, we will briefly look at it both from a doctrinal perspective and give a narrative overview.

"[We] get at the basics of a Christian worldview ... by discovering how it answers the three essential worldview questions."

Doctrinal Explanation of a Christian Worldview

From a doctrinal perspective, we get at the basics of a Christian worldview in the same way we get at the basics of any worldview system: we do it by discovering how it answers the three essential worldview questions. One must simply discover its authority source, then answer the three worldview questions based on that source. For the Christian faith, the foundational authority source is, of course, the Bible. So, we will now take a look at how the Bible answers the three essential worldview questions:

1. What is the nature of ultimate reality?
2. What is a human being?
3. What is the ultimate a person can achieve in this life?

What is the nature of ultimate reality? Who is God?

Obviously, in a Christian worldview, the God who is revealed in the Bible is understood to be the only true God. To explain what the Bible says about this particular subject in any kind of complete manner would require multiple volumes. In fact, there are scores of books that have already been written on this topic. Our purpose here is not to give that kind of comprehensive explanation, but to simply lay out the basics. Once you have a good sense of these basics, I would

> *"[In] a Christian worldview, the God who is revealed in the Bible is understood to be the only true God."*

recommend that you study other resources. We can never learn too much about who God has revealed himself to be.

In broad terms, we can examine the biblical understanding of God by looking at four basic categories:

> General Information about God,
> God the Father,
> God the Son, and
> God the Holy Spirit.

Let's briefly look at these topics.

General Information about God

1. There is One True and Living God. (Deuteronomy 6:4) The Christian faith is fiercely monotheistic. There is only one God and He is the God who has revealed Himself in the Bible.

2. God is Eternal. (Psalm 90:2) God's eternal existence cannot be fully understood or appreciated by those of us who are confined to a non-eternal material existence. That said, God has revealed Himself to have had no beginning and will have no end.

3. God is the Creator and Sustainer of the Universe. (Genesis 1:1, Hebrews 1:3) Before God created the material universe out of nothing, it simply did not exist. For His own purposes, He created it and He sustains its existence by His guiding hand.

4. God is Perfect. (2 Samuel 22:31) God has revealed Himself to be perfect in every way. There is no moral or any other kind of flaw in His person.

5. God is Worthy of Worship. (1 Timothy 1:17) Because of God's perfection, He is worthy of our absolute devotion to Him.

6. God is Spirit. (John 4:24) While God made human beings to be physical creatures, our essential essence transcends the physical and is spirit. This allows us to understand (to a degree) and connect with God who is spirit and, Himself, transcends physical reality.

7. God is Holy. (Leviticus 11:44) We have already mentioned God's perfection, but it is important to specifically cite the moral aspect of that perfection. Being holy, God is morally perfect. It is this moral perfection that becomes the model for the morality human beings are called to imitate.

8. God is a Trinity. (2 Corinthians 1:21-22) The concept of Trinity is a difficult one for human beings to fully grasp, because a Trinity cannot even exist based on the confining laws of the material universe. We know God to be a Trinity because He has revealed Himself this way. What this means is that, while He is one and only one God, within His being there are three completely separate persons (separate centers of consciousness) continuously communicating with each other. These three persons have been revealed to us as Father, Son, and Holy Spirit. While They are completely independent of each other as persons, They are perfectly unified in action and purpose within a single being.

9. God is a Person. (Exodus 6:2-4) Personhood describes the kind of being God is. Some people get confused with this descriptor because they associate personhood with human beings. However, that is not the way it works: God is the

original person, and the only reason human beings are persons is because He made us in His image. Personhood is a spiritual concept, not a physical one.

10. God Is a Spiritual Person. (John 4:24) To more fully understand the concept of personhood, it is important to grasp the elements that make it up. These are spiritual characteristics that make up the beings which can be characterized as persons:

- Knowledge. (1 Samuel 2:3) Knowledge relates to an individual's ability to acquire, store, and access information.
- Creativity. (Genesis 1:1) Creativity involves the use of an individual's imagination to create things.
- Personality. (Exodus 15:11) Personality relates to a person's unique characteristics that identify him as the person he is.
- Free Will. (Romans 12:2) Free-will creatures are able to determine what they want to do, and independently act in ways that accomplish that purpose.
- Gender. (Genesis 1:27) Gender is essentially a spiritual trait, not a physical one. It is the foundation of the ability to experience relationships. As a Trinitarian person, God contains the fullness of gender within Himself. As such, He is able to experience intimate relationship within Himself without resort to other beings.
- Eternalness. (Revelation 4:8) Eternalness, in the most comprehensive meaning of the word, means that there is no beginning and no end.
- Dominion. (1 Timothy 6:13-16) Dominion relates to a person's ability to exert control. As the source of everything, and specifically the creator of the material universe, God has

control over everything. He is the ultimate sovereign.

- Self-Consciousness. (Matthew 6:9-10) Self-consciousness is the ability to be aware of oneself. God is a person who is aware of His own existence and capable of contemplating His own purposes, as well as defining direction based on His self-interest.

11. Objective. (Romans 16:25-26) Objectivity relates to a person's actual existence as a being. God is not some nebulous spirit being that cannot be engaged. He is an objectively real person who can be known in an objectively real personal relationship.

12. Purposeful. (John 6:38-40) Purposefulness is expressed in a person's ability to act by intentional reasoning. God has a purpose which He is trying to accomplish in eternity and the material world. He is continually taking measures to see that it gets done.

13. Personal. (Hebrews 1:3) A personal creature is one that lives in relationship. The fact that God is a personal being has already been alluded to in several of the points above, but needs to be explicitly stated. As a person, He exists in relationship, and the ultimate purpose of His creative activity rests in relationship.

14. Character. Persons have character traits that define them. As a person, God has particular character traits and specifically does not have others. These, He has:

- Love. (1 John 4:8) Love is not merely something God does. It is an element of His very personhood. He cannot not love.
- Holiness. (Psalm 99:9) God is morally perfect. In fact, right morality is defined by His own moral perfection and is

revealed in the Bible.

- Mercy. (Daniel 9:9) Mercy refers to God's compassion and willingness to forgive those who rebel against Him. Because of our sin, human beings deserve judgment. God's mercy is a demonstration of His restraint, based on the fact that He doesn't fully give us what we deserve as we live life.
- Giving. (1 Timothy 6:17) God has determined to express His great love to mankind by giving blessings. In fact, God's kind of love gives without any expectation of return.
- Grace. (Ephesians 2:8) God's grace is expressed when He gives us blessings we do not deserve. It defines, more fully, one of the aspects of His giving nature.
- Kindness. (Psalm 25:8) Kindness is a character trait of God that is reflected in the benevolent actions He takes on behalf of His creation as we live life, as well as an expression of His love.
- Righteousness. (Daniel 9:14) God's righteousness is expressed in the fact that He always does what is right.
- Justice. (2 Thessalonians 1:4-10) As a person who is holy, God cannot allow sin to stand. Evil must be judged.
- Patience. (2 Peter 3:9) In spite of the fact that evil must be judged, God's great love inclines Him to have patience with human beings as we work out our salvation and grow in Him.

God the Father

Human fatherhood is a derivative of God's fatherhood, not the other way around. The true pattern of fatherhood is found in the perfection of God Himself. He is the ultimate model of fatherhood.

The truth is, God is a loving heavenly father, who is the Creator and Sustainer of the universe. He created human beings individually with a purpose to fulfill in life. He then made a way for us to know Him personally by providing a means by which we are able to enter into a personal relationship with Him as a very loved child. When we fully understand the person of God the Father, we have the kind of information about Him that gives us a reason to desire that relationship. There are four essential revealed characteristics of God the Father.

1. Creator. (Genesis 1:1) One of the most prominent aspects of God's fatherhood is revealed in His creative power. God is the source of all, and everything He created was for a purpose.
2. Sustainer. (Psalm 147:7-8) Not only has God created the material universe, He is active in keeping it going.
3. Interaction with Mankind. (Ephesians 3:14-15) The very concept of a father implies the personal. A man cannot be a father until there is a child. When a father has a child, there is inherent in that arrangement a personal relationship. So when God reveals Himself to mankind as Father, the inescapable implication is that a relationship exists.
4. Personal Relationship with Mankind. (John 1:12-13) While God does demonstrate His fatherly care over the entirety of His creation, that is not the ultimate expression of His fatherhood. That element is reserved for the father-child relationship He provides for those who choose to enter into a relationship with Him.

God the Son

Christ is the second person of the Trinity. As such, He is fully God. While we may not be able to understand this completely, based on God's revelation to us, there are a number of things we can know.

1. Christ as a Part of the Trinity. (John 20:28) In order to reveal Himself on earth as a human being, Christ had to limit Himself in ways that did not fully express His divinity. This limitation, though, only applied while He was manifested on earth as a man. As Christ in heaven, He is actually able to fully express Himself as God.

2. Christ as a Human Being. (Philippians 2:5-7) As Jesus, God revealed Himself in human flesh. But He was not a mere man. Rather, He was God, the Second Person of the Trinity, who put on human skin in order to dwell on earth.

3. The Life of Jesus. (Galatians 4:4) In order to accomplish God's purpose of salvation for mankind, it was necessary for there to be a sinless human being to become the atoning sacrifice for sin. As no mere human could accomplish this, God manifested Himself as a human being and did everything necessary by His life to fulfill His purpose.

4. The Death of Jesus. (Galatians 3:13) The death of Jesus occurred as a brutal execution, but it was not a mere execution. While His human persecutors intended it as such, this whole episode was God's plan from the beginning in order to accomplish the salvation of humanity. In fact, it was the very means by which God provided the way to heaven for mankind.

5. The Resurrection of Jesus. (Matthew 28:5-6) Once Christ died, He had to rise again. In doing this, He demonstrated that He had power over sin and death, and was able to actually accomplish salvation for humanity.
6. The Ascension of Jesus. (Mark 16:19) After the forty-day period when Jesus walked the earth following His resurrection, He ascended to heaven. In doing that, He returned to His rightful place in eternity as a part of the Godhead. There He serves as the intermediary between man and God, based on the work He did on earth as the ultimate sacrifice for sin.
7. The Return of Jesus. (1 Thessalonians 4:16-17) The second coming of Christ will mark the completion of the fix for the Fall. It will be an actual historical event and will be accomplished personally, bodily, and visibly. It will mark the end of the reign of sin in physical reality. At that point, Christ will judge the world and the new heaven and new earth will be instituted.

God the Holy Spirit

The third member of God's Trinitarian essence is the Holy Spirit. He is a person and is an integral part of the Godhead.

1. The Personhood of the Holy Spirit. (John 14:16-17) As a member of the Trinity, the Holy Spirit is God Himself. In order for God and man to enjoy a personal relationship, they must, somehow, be in proximity to one another. It is in the form of the Holy Spirit that God comes near as He indwells the body of every believer.
2. The Holy Spirit's Relationship to the Trinity. (John 16:13-15) The Holy Spirit is not a separate entity from the

Father and Christ. He is as fully One of the Persons of the Trinity as is the Father and the Son. As such, He is not a separate being from them, but He is a separate person.

3. The Role of the Holy Spirit in the Trinity. (John 14:26) The Bible teaches that God, in the form of the Holy Spirit, serves as the very presence of God in the believer. It also teaches that He is the source of all life; the one responsible for revealing truth to those who wrote the Scriptures; the illuminator of the minds of humans enabling them to understand the truth of Scripture; the convictor of those separated from Him by sin; the Comforter to give strength, peace, and guidance for living life; and the one who works in the lives of believers to call and equip them with gifts for service. Additionally, He was instrumental in the coming of Christ, as He caused Mary's impregnation, and goes out from the Father and the Son to accomplish the will and work of the Godhead in the world.

4. The Work of the Holy Spirit in the World. (Genesis 1:2) There are some instances in the Bible where God has manifested Himself in some kind of physical form. Most of the work done in the world by God, however, is attributed to the activity of the Holy Spirit. It is the Spirit who is the agent of God charged with carrying out the will of the Father and the Son in the world. It is the Spirit who inspired men to write Scripture. It is the Spirit who illuminates those who read Scripture in order to help them understand the will of God found in it.

5. The Work of the Holy Spirit with Non-Believers. (John 16:7-8) The Holy Spirit is the one who confronts individuals with their need for God as He creates conviction of sin within their hearts.

6. The Work of the Holy Spirit in the Believer. (Romans 8:11) In believers, the Holy Spirit baptizes individuals into union with Christ Himself, as well as into union with other believers in the Body of Christ. He also dwells continually within the life of every believer; acts within us as our intercessor before God and as our personal comforter; seals us into relationship with God to keep us from falling away; calls and qualifies believers for the work of ministry; reveals to us the deep things of God and guides us into all truth; enables us to accomplish the work of the kingdom; and endows us with the fruit of the Spirit.

What is a Human Being?

> *"It is in man that we see the characteristics of personhood explicitly expressed in life."*

The biblical understanding of man, in the Christian faith, is critical to an understanding of the overall character of God and our need for Him. It is in man that we see the characteristics of personhood explicitly expressed in life. It is also from this doctrine that our approach to living life and acquiring salvation comes into clear focus.

There are two aspects of our human existence that are critical to understand in this regard.

We are:

<u>Made in the Image of God</u> and
<u>Fallen</u>.

<u>Made in the Image of God</u> (Genesis 1:26 – 27)

Being made in the image of God simply means that man was created as a creature with the personhood characteristics of God. While human beings don't have these characteristics to the same degree God has them, we do have them to the extent that we can be characterized as persons. These image characteristics are spiritual in nature (see "God is a Spiritual Person" in the section above). This makes human beings creatures with special value; able to self-consciously interact with other persons.

<u>Fallen</u> (Genesis 3:1-13, 22-24)

When God created human beings, He created them without a sin nature. When Adam and Eve disobeyed God, however, sin was unleashed on the world. In mankind, this manifested itself in a sin nature that predisposes human beings to be rebellious against God. In this state we find ourselves separated from a holy God who will not fellowship with sin. It has caused us to be in need of a solution for the sin problem.

What Is the Ultimate a Person Can Achieve in this Life?
(Salvation)

"Christian salvation ... that begins at a point in time and continues from that moment through the rest of eternity."

The essence of Christian salvation cannot be described as an event. Rather it is a process that begins at a point in time and continues from that moment through the rest of eternity. A

biblical understanding of salvation is generally understood as consisting of three parts:
>Justification,
>Sanctification, and
>Glorification.

Justification (Romans 3:22-26)

The first stage of the salvation process is called justification, or the new birth. It takes place at a particular point in time when, by an act of faith, an individual repents of sin and acknowledges Christ as Savior and Lord. When an individual does this, God judicially declares the person not guilty of sin based on the death and resurrection of Jesus Christ. He then adopts the individual into His family.

Sanctification (Ephesians 4:11-13)

The second stage of the salvation process is referred to as sanctification. This phase begins at the point of justification, and continues for the rest of one's mortal life. During this time, believers demonstrate that their lives have actually been changed by God as they strive to live in an intimate relationship with Him. This relationship is expressed through a process of spiritual maturation.

Glorification (1 Corinthians 15:50-55)

The third and final stage of the salvation process is referred to as glorification and takes place at physical death. At that point the Christian leaves behind the physical body, with its sin nature, and enters directly into the presence of God to dwell with Him for eternity.

Narrative Description of a Christian Worldview

Gaining doctrinal knowledge and an understanding of the Christian worldview is very important. But a worldview is not just a doctrinal statement: it is personal, and actually plays out in history in an individual's life. As such, we need to understand the doctrine in the context of real life. A narrative description of the Christian worldview gives us this extra dimension of understanding.

"[A] worldview ... plays out in history in an individual's life. [We] we need to understand ... doctrine in the context of real life."

Creation

Nothing about the Christian faith can ultimately make any sense until we understand God's purpose in the creation. The beginning of the Christian story has its roots in the creation of mankind. Of course, before God created man in His own image, there were other created beings. These other beings, however, did not share the characteristic of being created in the image of God.

As a Trinitarian person, God is able to have an actual, viable relationship within His own personhood. In fact, relationship is a vital element of His very being. While He does not need any other creatures to fulfill His relationship need, He, at some point, decided to create another class of being that had the characteristics of personhood.

For His purpose to become a reality in actual existence, though, there had to be a place for this new person to live. So, God created the material universe, with Earth as the one place capable of sustaining the physical life of this new creature. Then, when it was ready, God created man and interacted with him as a physical being on this physical planet. He did this in order to share fellowship and fulfill His purpose for the creation.

The Fall

The concept of the Fall gets to the very heart of the human condition. It helps us understand our human nature and why human beings are separated from God.

In the beginning, God created mankind with the capability of interacting with Him in a loving, personal relationship. Initially, He and man enjoyed perfect fellowship as they interacted with each other in the earthly paradise He had created.

There came a time, though, when Adam and Eve willfully disobeyed God, and did the one thing that was able to break fellowship with Him. The result of this act introduced sin into the world and caused the destruction of the unrestricted fellowship that Adam and Eve had enjoyed with God. It also caused the degradation of the physical paradise itself. This evil penetrated the very core of humanity in general, and mankind's very nature became infected with sin. Every human person born since that time has inherited that sin nature. This sin nature predisposes individuals to think and act in ways that express sin through their lives. As a result, all human beings continue to find themselves separated from God because of this evil within.

Life after the Fall

After sin entered the world, it became the primary principle that ruled the universe. The ultimate result was that it broke the perfect creation God had made. It broke man's personal relationship with God as well as the very order of the physical universe itself.

Redemption

Redemption is the process God used to restore His fallen creation. Recognizing and understanding this fact is important because it is by God's redemptive plan that His salvation can be applied to our lives personally.

After the Fall, God could have chosen to destroy everything and start over. However, rather than allow Satan to win, God decided to overcome him and, in the process, fix (redeem) His creation. He would do this by providing mankind a means of salvation, and by ultimately creating a new heaven and new earth from the carcass of the old.

To do this, God began a process which would reverse the effects of sin that were introduced at the Fall. This process began with God's decision to send a redeemer into the world who would offer Himself as a sacrifice in place of those who found themselves separated from God because of their sin. This redeemer would have to be a person who would be completely without sin, and thus worthy of standing in this position. As no other being was qualified, God determined that He Himself would become the redeemer.

As the history of the earth moved forward, God continuously revealed to mankind how to know this relationship with Himself.

Then, with the death of Christ on the cross, God actually fulfilled the work of redeemer to make the possibility of salvation a reality. Then, with His resurrection from the dead, He demonstrated that He actually had the power to accomplish this task. With that, the completion of the redemptive process was sealed.

Eternity

In the beginning of this section, we noted that everything begins with an understanding of the purpose of God. Nothing in the story of the Christian faith makes any sense until we understand why God did what He did in making His creation. Once we understand that, the culmination of God's plan begins to make sense.

When we examine God's plan for the redemption of mankind, we see that it works itself out in a three-step process. It all began in the mind of God, and was put into effect at His instigation through the creation of the world and of mankind. But the ultimate outworking of His plan is expressed in the life of individual human beings, based on the decisions they make during their life on earth.

Those who receive God's salvation will enter eternity in relationship with Him. Additionally, when the fullness of God's timing is accomplished, He will also restore the material universe as a "new heaven and new earth." He will do that to fulfill His original plan. With that, all of the believers who had been brought into the presence of God at their physical death, will be resurrected to the new earth and given resurrected bodies. All of these people will then begin to dwell in this new condition on a physical earth, for eternity, as God had originally intended.

There are, of course, many details about the new heaven and new earth not specifically revealed in Scripture. God has, however, shared with us the big picture as we have seen here. In the end, He will have completely overcome the destructive attempt of Satan to disrupt His creation. The effects of sin will have been overcome, and the created order, as God intended it, will emerge fully developed. He will have His created world, and a class of eternal Kingdom citizens, who will personally interact and engage Him in a mutually loving relationship throughout the rest of eternity.

The Structure of Reality

"[We've] said before, reality is structured in some objectively real way and it is not structured in any other way. That way is reflected in what has been revealed in the Bible."

As we've said before, reality is structured in some objectively real way and it is not structured in any other way. That way is reflected in what has been revealed in the Bible.

To understand this, we need to understand what the Bible teaches about how to answer the three essential worldview questions. This gives us a doctrinal explanation of how that structure is organized. In order to get a full grasp of this, we need to also understand the big-picture context of the doctrines. With this explanation now in hand, we are in a position grasp what reality actually looks like.

Discussion Questions

1. What does the Bible teach about God?
2. What does the Bible teach about humanity?
3. What does the Bible teach about salvation?
4. Based on a narrative description, what is the big-picture context of reality?

Consider this ...

- "If you don't believe in tongues, you are not an authentic Christian."
- "If you don't believe in predestination, you are not a true Christian."
- "If you don't believe in Christ's return based on premillennial dispensationalism, you don't believe the Bible."
- "If you don't believe that Israel continues today to be God's chosen people, you will not be blessed by God."
- "If you will just give sacrificially to "X" ministry, God will bless you financially."

All of these are quotes I have heard in many different places. Those who say these things are generally very sincere, but are they true? And whether they are true or not, does it really make any difference?

What do you make of the fact that different Christian groups believe different things?

Chapter XIX

Why Christians Believe Different Things
WHICH DENOMINATION IS THE RIGHT ONE?

As I interact with Christians in various places and situations, there often emerges a great deal of lament about the fact that there is so little Christian unity. Of course, whenever this topic comes up, it is interesting to me that the laments of different Christian individuals are not always about the same thing. Some of them are truly distressed that Christians don't seem able to get along with each other. Others lament the fact that churches appear to have a difficult time cooperating with each other on various projects. Still others are troubled that there are so many different denominations.

Even non-Christians will often try to use the lack of Christian unity to denigrate Christians and Christianity. Some even point to the existence of many denominations as a means of attempting to prove that there is no such thing as a "true" Christian faith. Others use this argument to try and justify their own relativistic philosophy.

"[Know] where to draw the line between what is and is not authentic Christianity and ... how to make those distinctions."

The truth is, much of the lack of unity is truly problematic. On the other hand, some of it is not a lack of unity at all: unity in the Christian faith does not necessarily mean unification of organizations or uniformity of style. The issue that is actually most critical is to know where to draw the line between what is and is not authentic Christianity, and to know how to make those distinctions.

Essentials

Much of what people point to as a lack of unity among Christians really has nothing to do with the core beliefs of the Christian faith at all. It has, rather, to do with personal preferences and non-essential beliefs. To fully understand this, we must first make the distinction between beliefs that are essential to the Christian faith and those that are not.

As we have seen in previous chapters, there is a line that can be drawn around every belief system that defines its outer boundaries. Anything inside the line belongs to that belief system. But cross it and you have moved out of that system into something entirely different. Along with that, it must be acknowledged that within a single system, there can be a lot of—variety. This principle applies to every belief system in existence —including our Christian faith.

> *"[There] is a line that can be drawn around every belief system that defines its outer boundaries."*

This issue is difficult for some to understand because it often relates to how people interpret the Bible. In order to address this more fully, let's review the essential beliefs that create the outer boundary of the Christian faith. From there we can make some important distinctions.

The essential beliefs of a belief system are expressed by the three essential worldview questions:

1) What is the nature of ultimate reality?
2) What is a human being?
3) What is the ultimate that human beings can gain in this life?

The Christian faith answers these three questions in its own particular way.

1) Ultimate reality is expressed as the God of the Bible (holy, just, love, Trinity).
2) Human beings are persons created in the image of God, but fallen.
3) The ultimate that human beings can gain in this life (salvation) is to enter into a personal, eternal relationship with God based on the death and resurrection of Jesus Christ.

Every authentic, biblical Christian will answer these three essential questions the same way—regardless of denomination, culture, location, or any other factor.

Non-Essentials

There are other matters and issues that are a part of life and of religious experience which must be dealt with outside these three questions. While every true believer will answer the essential questions the same way, there can be a massive amount

---

"One source of disunity can be traced to a difference in style preferences."

---

of variety related to the other matters and issues. Let's take a look at some of the possibilities related to this variety.

Preferences

One source of disunity can be traced to a difference in style preferences. So as we look at our Christian faith, we can see that many of the differences people point to as divisive are actually nothing more than differing style preferences. This can include such things as organizational structure, music tastes, the way people express worship, and the like. Sadly, these preferences can lead to a lot of conflict and division among various groups of Christians. That said, there is nothing related to style that affects a person's relationship with God. Everything related to style preferences is a matter non-essential to the faith.

Non-Essential Beliefs

There is a second cause for disunity that is a bit more difficult to get at. This one has to do with non-essential beliefs. Many beliefs arise from the way people interpret the Bible that relate to questions outside the three essentials. These may pertain to issues such as eschatology (last things/end times), the meaning and practice of baptism and the Lord's Supper, speaking in tongues, predestination, the proper day of the week to worship, whether or not women should wear makeup, the role of men and women in church life, and many others. It is not that these issues are unimportant, or even that there are not actual right and wrong interpretations: it is just that in the case of every non-essential, even if you are wrong it does not put you outside the faith. It can skew the way you practice your faith and affect your relationships with other people, but it doesn't push you outside of a relationship with God.

"[But with] every <u>non-essential</u>, even if you are wrong—<u>it does not put you outside the faith</u>."

That said, many people latch onto particular non-essential beliefs as if they were essential, and treat those who hold different beliefs about their pet non-essential belief as *persona non grata*. So, it is this kind of situation that is at the root of many elements of disunity. This kind of disunity may have significant, sometimes even profound, effects on how Christians interact with one another. But make no mistake, that effect is purely temporal and has no bearing on how God evaluates the acceptance of a person into His kingdom.

Non-Biblical Lifestyles

There is another category that relates to unity among Christians we must also address. This category is extremely serious and relates either to ignorance of the Christian faith or deliberate rebellion against God. There are many who self-identify as Christians (either because they were born in America, were baptized as children or youth, or because their name is on a church roll), but who live life based on a set of worldview beliefs that extend beyond the boundaries of authentic Christianity. This includes, for instance, people who claim to be Christians but live an immoral lifestyle (cohabitation, same sex relationship, lack of integrity, etc.), or who simply believe non-Christian beliefs (naturalistic evolution, acceptance of abortion, homosexual marriage, *etc.*). In these cases, an individual's lifestyle and affirmations betray actual beliefs, that do not correspond with an authentic Christian faith.

The reason this is important is because true Christian salvation is not simply an intellectual belief or a self-identity. It is, literally, a changed life. Salvation involves not only a profession of faith that leads to justification, but also a changed life that leads to a godly lifestyle (sanctification). When a person receives Christ into his or her life, God enters that life and creates a change. He establishes an objectively real, new nature that ignites within the individual a desire to be intimate with God. This desire compels one to put aside sin and false beliefs. People who hold on to their prior immoral lifestyles and non-biblical beliefs are giving indication that their lives were never changed, and that God does not, in reality, dwell within.

> ## "In truth, only God and the individual knows whether the life change has ever taken place."

This is not meant to judge other people. In truth, only God and the individual knows whether the life change has ever taken place. That said, a person's core beliefs produce a particular lifestyle; and when it is evident that a particular lifestyle is not producing godly fruit, is likely that the person's master is not God.

When it comes to Christian unity, those who call themselves Christians but live life as if they are not Christians, are not going to participate in the faith life of the body of Christ. Their hypocrisy also defames the church as it gives militant anti-Christians ammunition to attack Christian beliefs.

"[There] are entire theologies that claim to be Christian but which simply are not."

Non-Christian "Christian" Theologies

A final reason we see divisions in the Christian faith is that there are entire theologies that claim to be Christian but which simply are not. Churches or groups that adhere to these theological approaches do not even make a pretense to believe the three essential worldview beliefs that characterize biblical Christianity. Typically, these groups fall into one of two categories.

The first category is comprised of belief systems that started out Christian, but over time adopted a non-biblical theology. The most common of these are Christian denominations that have adopted liberal theological beliefs such as neo-orthodoxy, liberation theology, or postmodern theology. Many of these theologies do not even acknowledge the supernatural, or at the very least do not believe that the Bible gives a true understanding of what that might look like. These kinds of groups still hold on to a Christian denominational identity, but no longer hold any Christian content.

The second category is composed of groups that we would identify as cults. These do typically believe in a supernatural reality. In fact, some of them actually borrow beliefs and concepts from Christianity, but have developed other beliefs that have no correspondence whatsoever with biblical Christianity. Many of these actually claim to be the only authentic Christian faith. This category might include such groups as Mormons, Jehovah's Witnesses, Unity, and others.

The Right "Different" is Okay

In truth, true Christians do divide themselves up based on their preferences for particular approaches to worship,

> ## "True Christians are all members of the body of Christ and are spiritual siblings."

various demographics, and even certain non-essential beliefs. Sadly, some even shun fellowship with other authentic Christians based on these differences. In cases like that, what we are witnessing is an attitude problem, not a belief problem.

True Christians are all members of the body of Christ and are spiritual siblings. We all have the same Heavenly Father and are all part of the same spiritual family. On the other hand, I believe the majority in this category do recognize, even if at a superficial level, that non-essential beliefs should not prevent fellowship with other believers.

"[Non-essential] beliefs should not prevent fellowship with other believers."

Discussion Questions

1. What are the essentials of the Christian faith?
2. What kinds of non-essentials still tend to divide Christians and how can this be avoided?
3. What evidence exists that some who call themselves Christians are not?

Consider this ...

Occasionally I write an article or make a video about some hot-button social issue and express the Christian belief about that topic. And when I do that, it is not unusual for me to come under attack by people who don't believe in the Christian faith. As I engage this kind of discussion, I actually try to get away from talking about the particular social issue as quickly as I can. The reason for this is that the real problem is not with any particular social issue. Rather, it is with the underlying beliefs that affirm the "rightness" or "wrongness" of people's beliefs about the issue.

A pro-abortion person, for instance, is not really that interested in abortion. Typically, the real issue has to do with justifying a lifestyle that allows for sexual promiscuity or personal freedom. That, to them, is more important than the life they may create by their sexual activity. A homosexual marriage advocate is not really interested in homosexual marriage, as much as in justifying a homosexual lifestyle. When dealing with these and other issues that cause controversies in the culture, one must operate below the surface—at the worldview level—in order to actually deal with their root causes.

What is the difference between a worldview conflict and a belief system conflict?

Chapter XX

What Does Worldview Conflict Look Like?
Cat Fight!!!!!

We hear a lot these days about the "culture wars." But what are they, really? We see it expressed, for instance, in the abortion debate and the battle over homosexual marriage. But culture wars are not "things" you can physically manipulate. Rather, they are the outward expression of ideas that are in conflict with one another. When we think of culture wars, what we are really dealing with are the outward expressions of beliefs that have much deeper roots. In truth, culture wars are the outward expression of the more deeply held conflicting worldview beliefs. Before there is ever any outward expression, there is an inner belief that fuels what we see outwardly.

"If you want to ... really make a difference, you have to change hearts and minds. And to do that, you must convince people to examine their worldview beliefs."

When you see the fight in the culture over abortion or homosexual marriage, the fight is not actually about those issues. The fight is really about the underlying beliefs that support the different points of view. If you only fight the battle at the level of the culture wars, you basically never get beyond one opinion battling another. The only possible result of that is the victory of the one who can win the PR battle or the power struggle. If you want to get to the place where you can really make a difference, you have to change hearts and minds. And to do that, you must convince people to examine their worldview beliefs.

Issues That *The Truth Mirage* Engages

We have already mentioned a couple of the more prominent issues that are front and center in modern America's culture war—abortion and homosexual marriage. But there are so many more. In fact, most people would not recognize some of them to even be a part of this discussion. Differences over matters related to such things as sexual morality, economics, political philosophy, the nature of humanity, beliefs about biology, and even belief about what is the most important thing a person can gain out of life, are also expressions of worldview conflict.

The reason these outward "culture war" issues get so much traction in our discussions is because these are the things that are easy to identify and that can be fought over in the political arena, in our educational institutions, and in the various pop culture venues. By passing legislation, teaching certain points of view in schools, and expressing particular points of view in music, movies, and television, it is possible to create the illusion that we are taking on and defeating points of view that oppose our own. So, the hot topic issues come

"[When] two people with different worldview beliefs engage a conversation, they end up talking right past one another without even realizing it."

front and center; generating a lot of heat but little light. For the truth is, dealing only with these surface issues will never help us uncover the root of the problem.

The Nature of Worldview Disputes

As we have already discussed thoroughly, worldview beliefs, for most people, are unconscious. They are unconscious because they are, literally, the way people understand how reality exists. It generally does not dawn on the average person that it is even possible for other people to view reality differently than they do. After all, how could anyone consider something real that you "know" to be a fantasy. But that is exactly what is going on in American culture. As such, when two people with different worldview beliefs engage a conversation, they end up talking right past one another without even realizing it. Even if they are using the same vocabulary to talk about their issues, what they mean when the use those words is entirely different.

To help clarify this thought, let's take a look at one example. This could be multiplied over and over again on virtually any topic, but hopefully you will get the picture with this single illustration.

Let's take the issue of abortion, for instance. This debate is generally engaged with one side believing abortion is okay and the other side believing it is not. But typically, even the side that wants to allow abortion will not actually say abortion is a good thing. In fact, one of the common pro-abortion expressions is that it should be "safe, legal, and rare." The only problem is, specific efforts to make it "safe" by banning certain dangerous procedures or requiring more medical oversight are fought against tooth and nail by the pro-abortionists. By the same token, efforts to enact requirements that would help make it more "rare" are also adamantly opposed. In fact, every restriction that is ever proposed is contested.

Beyond that, those who support abortion try not to even use the term "pro-abortion"—instead, they are "pro-choice." Rather than even deal with the question of abortion, they try to turn it into an issue regarding control over one's own body. Based on their worldview perspective, the real issue at hand is freedom and personal autonomy. In their view, the issue of personal autonomy trumps life.

The anti-abortion side, on the other hand, sees abortion as the killing (murder) of an innocent child. In fact, to counter the "pro-choice" concept of the other side, they will often use the term "pro-life." In their view, the issue of life trumps the issue of choice.

As we look deeper into this, it really is not simply a clash between different choices people make. It is actually a clash of beliefs about the nature of life itself.

> *"[It] really is not simply a clash between different choices people make. It is actually a clash of beliefs about the nature of life itself."*

One side believes the life and preferences of the woman are primary, while the other side believes the life of an innocent child is primary. The pro-abortion advocates base their case on the belief that a pre-born child is not really even a person, but is only a piece of tissue. This belief is based on a naturalistic worldview; which does not acknowledge the existence of a supernatural reality. They believe human beings are simply one species of natural animal among many, and that human life is no more valuable than any other life form. They also believe that since there is no supernatural reality, there is no God to reveal what is right and what is wrong. As such, human beings have to make up their own morality. And what they make up is based on what they perceive to be best for them at any given time.

The other side believes that human life is special because humans were created by God

"So, there you have the worldview clash ... about what beliefs represent actual reality, ... not about the outward expression of the beliefs."

and in His image. This belief in God acknowledges that He is the author of life, and it is not the prerogative of other human beings to destroy innocent human life. Beyond that, they believe God has revealed to man the fact that human life is valuable, and to destroy innocent human life is immoral.

So, there you have the worldview clash. It is not really about abortion *per se*. Rather, it is about what beliefs represent actual reality. Does God exist? And if He does, did He create human beings to be special? Do human beings have the right to destroy innocent human life or not? The real fight is about people's beliefs concerning reality, not about the outward expression of the beliefs.

As it turns out, a person's worldview beliefs are the most basic beliefs he or she holds. They are so basic that if they are upset, it literally turns a person's life upside down. It is so basic that when a person changes from one set of worldview beliefs to another, it constitutes a religious conversion. As such, people don't give up their worldview beliefs very easily. When you

"Ultimately, the only way this war ends is for one side to win and the other side to lose ... by using intimidation and force [—or—by converting] people to a different worldview belief."

challenge a person's worldview beliefs, they will typically react against you: this is the root of *The Truth Mirage*.

Ultimately, the only way this war ends is for one side to win and the other side to lose. There are a couple of ways this happens.

One way is by using intimidation and force. The problem with this approach is that the conversion may not be at all sincere. When threatened, some people may convert outwardly without actually taking on different worldview beliefs. When true conversion does not take place, an individual may be silenced for a time, but the root of the fight still exists. As the situation evolves over time and opportunities arise, the fight will be resumed. Brute force is only a temporary solution, and the fallout is always destroyed lives.

The other way to win the culture war is to share a different worldview in a fashion convincing enough that you are actually able to convert people to a different worldview belief. This approach requires not only knowing what you believe, but also why it is the truth. Ultimately, the "why" question must be answered. In an ultimate sense, conversion is the only approach that is capable of actually winning; because it is the only one that changes hearts and minds.

Discussion Questions

1. How do culture wars express themselves as a Truth Mirage?
2. To really understand the issues that are fought over in the culture wars, what is necessary?
3. How can culture wars actually be won?

Consider this ...

In our day, there are quite a few very well-known politicians, in the highest echelons of government, who adamantly maintain that they are Christians in the face of massive criticism by evangelicals. These politicians all claim to be pro-abortion and pro-gay marriage. In addition, they pick sides regarding race relations, put down Christians and Christianity, don't believe the Bible to be a revelation from God, favor Islam over Christianity, frequently tell blatant lies, use the government bureaucracy to oppress Christians and political opponents, and ignore the law they swore to uphold and protect. So, the question becomes, are these people really Christians?

What is the bottom line necessity for being a genuine Christian?

Chapter XXI

Evaluating the Truth of Theism
DO YOU WANT THE RED PILL OR THE BLUE PILL?

A s I interact with various Christians about what is going on in the world and about how Christians should respond to it, one of the things I commonly see is doubt and uncertainty. Some of the uncertainty relates to how Christians ought to speak about various social issues. Other doubt relates to how they ought to act toward people who think differently than they. But much of it is actually about the beliefs themselves. In a relativistic world with so many ideas on the table, how can we know the beliefs we hold actually reflect a biblical worldview?

> *"[How] can we know the beliefs we hold actually reflect a biblical worldview?"*

To deal with this topic, we need to look at two elements. The first is doctrinal: there truly are beliefs that define the parameters of a biblical worldview. Hold to those and you are genuinely a Christian. Deviate from them, and you have stepped out of Christianity. The second element relates to lifestyle. People's beliefs are not merely what they profess verbally. True beliefs are actually played out in life. Let's take a look at these two topics to clarify what a biblical worldview really looks like.

What You Believe about the Three Worldview Questions

Every belief system in existence, whether at the worldview level or the belief system level, has some authority source it depends on to define its parameters. In the case of a biblical worldview, that authority source is the Bible. If something is taught in the Bible, it reflects some element of a biblical worldview. If the belief being considered is contrary to biblical teaching, it does not reflect a biblical worldview.

Of course, as we have clearly seen earlier, there are points of dispute among honest, Bible believing Christians. But, as we have also noted, legitimate disagreements relate only to non-essential beliefs.

"[A person's faith essentials] are defined by how a person answers the three essential worldview questions."

Every true Christian will believe the same thing about the faith's essentials; and these essentials are defined by how a person answers the three essential worldview questions. So, if you answer these three questions the way the Bible answers them, you hold a biblical worldview—regardless of any disagreements you may have with other believers concerning non-essential beliefs. Just to clarify this point, let's review how the Bible answers the three essential worldview questions.

1. What Is the Nature of Ultimate Reality?

A biblical worldview points to the God of the Bible as the foundation for ultimate reality. In particular, the Bible teaches that God exists as a Trinitarian being (one God in three persons) Who is holy, just, and love—all three of these at the same time, too.

2. *What is a Human Being?*

The Bible teaches that man is a special creation of God who was created in His image but is fallen. As creatures created in His image, we are special in that we have, as a part of our being, the personhood characteristics of God Himself. This special status places a high value on human life. But mankind is also fallen. We have, as a part of our very existence, a sin nature that gives us a tendency to rebel against God. This rebellion creates separation from Him that must be rectified.

3. *What Is the Ultimate a Human Being Can Get Out of this Life?* (Salvation)

In biblical terminology, the question regarding the ultimate human beings can get out of life becomes, "What is salvation?" Since mankind is separated from God, because of human fallenness, something must be done to repair the damage the sin problem has created. God's original purpose for the creation of mankind was for Him to be able to enjoy an intimate personal relationship with humanity. Salvation is, then, the restoration of that relationship.

Biblical salvation is based on the principle of substitutionary atonement (a person who is not guilty of sin taking the punishment for the sin of the one who is guilty) because human beings are not capable of individually meeting the requirements to have their sin forgiven. God provided this salvation based on His love for and grace on behalf of sinful man. He did it by the death and resurrection of Jesus Christ.

Finally, salvation is received by individuals when they open their lives to Christ by placing their faith in Him for their salvation. When human beings do this, they receive the ultimate this life has to offer—entry into a personal relationship with God by being adopted into His family.

Doctrinally, the answer to these three questions defines a biblical worldview. Thus, those who believe this way can be said to have a biblical worldview.

How You Live Your Life

While there are specific doctrinal beliefs that correspond to every worldview, there are

> *"[Every] person will always live by their worldview beliefs."*

also corresponding lifestyle components. A worldview is a set of beliefs that actually define how a person understands reality to exist. Individuals cannot live outside what they believe is real. As such, every person will always live by their worldview beliefs.

This does not mean they will necessarily live by the worldview beliefs that they *claim* to follow. In fact, when it comes to lifestyle, there are many people who claim to be Christians but live "as if" the teachings of the Bible are not true. In these cases, the person's profession simply does not reflect the actual worldview beliefs they hold. For instance, when you come across a person who says they believe the Bible, yet are living with another person outside of marriage, their profession doesn't match their lifestyle. In actuality, that person does not hold a biblical worldview. There is something about their beliefs that permits them to live in ways which literally contradict what the Bible teaches. The same is true about those who believe in naturalistic evolution or advocate for abortion. These are anti-Bible beliefs, and those who advocate for them are not advocating a biblical worldview.

A person will ALWAYS live out their worldview! If they claim one belief but live by another, it is the one they live by that is their actual worldview belief. So, look at the actions you take in life and see if they match up with biblical worldview beliefs. If you find that there isn't a match in some areas, it is evident that in those areas you do not hold a biblical worldview.

Living Out a Biblical Worldview

When it comes to living out a biblical worldview, there are some things that are going to be the same for every person. This sameness relates specifically to beliefs and motivations. Every person who truly holds a biblical worldview will believe, from the heart, what the Bible teaches about the three essential worldview questions. This will be outwardly expressed in life as individuals love what God loves, and hate what God hates. It will be expressed further as they put God and his kingdom above earthly motivations. Finally, it will be expressed as believers look for opportunities to share their faith with those who are outside of a relationship with God.

Biblical worldview beliefs will also, in some ways, be expressed differently in different people based on their calling and gifting. There are those God calls to be leaders in the church and others he calls to serve Him in other capacities. There are people He calls to be out front confronting the culture, and those who need to be working behind the scenes. There are those who live out

"A biblical worldview is centered on God and His will."

their faith in the culture in one profession as opposed to another. Further, everyone has been specifically given spiritual gifts by God to enable them to perform particular kinds of ministry. God gives each individual a distinct calling to impact a particular element of culture.

A biblical worldview is centered on God and His will. Those who truly believe God exists as He is described in the Bible, and who have come to actually know Him in a personal relationship, will live life based on that understanding of reality.

Discussion Questions

1. How does the Bible answer the three essential worldview questions?
2. What does a person's lifestyle tell you about their worldview beliefs?
3. How does God work in individual believer's lives to equip them to carry out his will in daily life?

Consider this ...

In the summer of 2014, ISIS gained control of most of the northern part of the country of Iraq. In the first year after that invasion, because of their violence and threats, more than 125,000 of Iraq's Christians were forced to flee the land their ancestors had lived in for nearly 2,000 years. In spite of the persecution and intentional killing of Christians, these faithful believers refused to renounce their faith.

Two years after Oregon Christian bakers Melissa and Aaron Klein refused to make a wedding cake for a homosexual wedding, the owners of Sweet Cakes by Melissa faced threats, heavy fines, and the loss of their constitutional rights. In spite of that, they refused to be bullied into putting aside their faith.

While these kinds of things are happening all around, not all Christians are just sitting back and letting it happen. Obviously, there are people fighting back. But what can a regular person do?

What has God directed you to do
to stand strong for your faith
in Christ?

Chapter XXII

How Can Christians Effectively Fight the Worldview War?
You don't have to be on the defensive about your faith.

T he war for the heart and soul of America is becoming increasingly strident, and Christians are being attacked in unprecedented ways. The most visible expressions of this war are what we see going on in the culture. One place we see it is in the persecution of Christians who stand up for their Christian beliefs concerning sexual morality. People are being fired from their jobs, fined, and actually having their businesses shut down for not participating in certain events, or even for simply criticizing non-biblical lifestyles. The rationale being used to justify this persecution is the claim that Christians are illegally discriminating against people.

The fact is, though, this is simply not true. It is, certainly, viewed that way by the anti-Christian crowd: but in order to come to that conclusion, it becomes necessary to evaluate the morality of various actions through a set of worldview beliefs that, in the end, simply do not logically hold up. That doesn't matter, though, because the logic of the detractors seems logical to them. It is *The Truth Mirage* that they see. And to the extent they hold the levers of power, they are able to enforce their will. As such, the outward expressions of this war are overtly political.

While the outward expression is political, the root of the battle is not political at all — it is spiritual. When you get to the bottom line, what is going on is a battle for hearts and minds. It is a battle for truth.

"The process of making a real difference ... must be done by education and a change of heart."

That being the case, there is a place for political action. But it is very important to understand that political action is only a stopgap measure. It is a matter of putting one's finger in the proverbial dike until the structure of the dike itself can be shored up.

The process of making a real difference is not one that can be addressed via political action. It must be done by education and a change of heart. Let's look at what is really involved in this process.

Knowledge

One of the greatest shortcomings of Christians these days is ignorance—ignorance of the context of the worldview war and of the basics of their own Christian faith. A person cannot intelligently believe what is not understood. By the same token, it is impossible to explain to another what one does not know. There is a knowledge base that must be grasped. It must be grasped to the degree that we become confident in our own faith. Furthermore, it must give us the ability to explain that faith to non-believers. Remember, they truly believe *The Truth Mirage* they hold onto.

Most of the conversation done in the world today is in sound bites. Unfortunately, sound bites have very little explanatory power. You can attack and put people down, as well as rally the troops, using sound bites—but you cannot explain anything complex. When dealing with an issue as complex as worldview, explanation is required. Worldview relates to the assumptions people make about the nature of reality. How can you possibly explain reality without providing a more in-depth explanation? You can't!

"With this knowledge, a Christian is able to have confidence in his or her own faith along with the ability to point out the flaws of other faith systems."

So, one of the first things Christians must possess is a willingness to make the effort to learn the foundational concepts of worldview. This involves a general understanding of the basic concept of worldview; the foundational presuppositions of the four basic worldviews; along with a more in-depth understanding of the Christian worldview. This means learning about *The Truth Mirage* other people are seeing. It also involves an explanation of why our Christian faith really does represent the truth about reality. This knowledge is not outside the reach of the everyday Christian, but it will take more effort and commitment than the average Christian is willing to put forth. With this knowledge, a Christian is able to have confidence in his or her own faith along with the ability to point out the flaws of other faith systems.

Skills

In addition to a basic knowledge foundation, Christians also need certain skill sets. There is one skill in particular that everyone needs to master, and others that will be relevant to particular individuals.

"[The] ability to communicate the gospel message across worldview ... has now become necessary for the everyday Christian, even in America."

The one that everyone must master is how to share the gospel message. At some point, a nonbeliever must be presented the opportunity to receive Christ if they are ever going to enter into a personal relationship with God. In the past, one could get away with only knowing how to explain the gospel message itself. Of course, that is still an essential part of the mix and that message has never changed.

But there is another element that has become increasingly necessary: the ability to communicate the gospel message across worldview barriers—to speak into the mirage of non-believers. This particular skill used to be most necessary for missionaries who worked in places dominated by other worldview systems. With the massive pluralization of American culture, though, this skill has now become necessary for the everyday Christian, even in America. As you should be able to see, this skill is built solidly upon the basic knowledge foundation referred to above.

Essentially, this skill is the ability to explain our faith in ways that make sense to whoever is hearing the message. And this explanation will be different depending on the worldview background of the person with whom one is interacting. For instance, if you are dealing with a Naturalist, you must be able to explain that God really is an objectively real person. If dealing with an Animist, you must be able to explain that there is only one God. At this point we are not talking about an explanation of the gospel message itself. We are dealing with communication skills that allow us to share our message with people who see reality in an entirely different way than our Christian point of view—in a way that speaks into their mirage.

But even after an individual has mastered the cross-worldview communication skill, it is still necessary to have the ability to explain the gospel message itself. As can be seen, the necessary skill and knowledge base are not completely separate. They must work together.

"[Every] Christian should discern his or her spiritual gift(s), and develop the associated skills in order to be effective in taking the gospel message out into the world."

There is also another category of skills Christians need to master—skills related to one's spiritual gifts. God has called every believer to be a minister of the gospel. But that calling will be exercised in many different venues, and in many different ways. Only a handful of people, relatively speaking, are called into church leadership; and people who have that calling must master the skills related to that work. But everyone is called to be a missionary somewhere. So, in addition to the skills related to sharing the gospel, every Christian should discern his or her spiritual gift(s), and develop the associated skills in order to be effective in taking the gospel message out into the world. If every believer did that, the message would spread quickly and powerfully.

Develop a Plan

Another thing Christians must do in order to effectively break into a non-believer's mirage is to become intentional: the work of God through people's lives doesn't just happen. It happens when individuals commit themselves to him and put forth the effort to make it happen. That requires a plan.

> *"Christians must ... become intentional, ... must confront people with the truth of the gospel, and [must] lead them to faith in Him."*

It must be remembered, first and foremost, that the plan must be directed in a particular direction. That direction relates to the accomplishment of God's purposes in the world — to bring people to Christ. That plan will, of course, be expressed differently in each person's life.

For some people, the plan will involve political activism. As mentioned earlier, though, political activism is not an end in itself. The end is always spiritual and is designed to bring people into relationship with Christ. The political work can only be a means to that end. We all live in an environment that either promotes what is right or promotes an agenda that leads away from that which is right. Political work is the work of creating an environment. There are believers who are called by God to work in the political arena; to help create an environment that allows the work of God to be more easily and effectively carried out. It must be remembered, though, that even if the environment is created rightly, that does not necessarily mean God's ultimate purpose gets accomplished. It is not the government's job to do the work of God. That is the job of believers. It is up to believers to take advantage of the free environment the government creates to do God's work.

This, then, brings us to the main point: no matter what arena we are working in, whether political or some other, the ultimate purpose of God is spiritual. It can only be accomplished by developing and fulfilling plans that are directed toward carrying out God's spiritual purpose. Our plans must confront people with the truth of the gospel and lead them to faith in Him.

It is not our responsibility, as human beings, to draw people into relationship with God. We do not have that ability. We are only God's messengers to share the message of His love. When we do, it is then up to Him to reveal Himself to them — to break through their mirage so they can see the real truth. At that point, each individual must make a personal decision as to whether or not they will open their hearts to Him.

Into the Fire

As essential as it is to prepare oneself to deal with the conflicting beliefs that will be encountered in the culture, none of it has any meaning if the knowledge, skills, and plans are not taken out into the world and used as instruments to accomplish the purpose of God. God's purpose for mankind is that we live in relationship with Him. He personally confronts the heart of every individual. But He has also commissioned believers to be instruments in His hand to share His message.

If we are going to be faithful in carrying out our calling, we have to be willing to walk into the fire. It is not enough to become educated, trained, and to develop a plan, we must also carry out the plan. We have to put ourselves in a position where our faith in God and our commitment to serve Him is more important to us than whatever it is we might lose by standing strong. We must become willing to charge the gates of hell with a water pistol.

Of course, God's calling on the lives of individuals comes with a great deal of variety. On one extreme there are those he has called to be martyrs. And in some parts of the world that is a horrible reality, even today. On the other extreme, there are those He wants to put into positions of influence behind the scenes; where they will be able to express the gospel in ways that don't draw oppositional attention. Most people, though, will have to live with various levels of tension between the two extremes. Regardless of the specifics of any individual's situation, it is important to be intentional in expressing the gospel in ways that accomplish the purpose of God through one's calling.

Contrary to the theology of certain preachers and evangelists, God's purpose in the world is not to make us rich and satisfied. His purpose is to bring the world into relationship with Himself.

And for us to find our place in His plan, we must put ourselves under His lordship—however that plays out in our individual lives. Our hope is in eternity, not in this temporal world. The ultimate blessings of God only come when we are living in relationship with Him. Living out a biblical worldview means

---

"God has given believers the task of speaking into the many truth mirages in order that His will can be done on earth as it is in heaven."

---

having our lives fully conformed to God and His ways: this is the only place where we will find the deepest fulfillment it is possible to have in life.

We live in a world full of people who hold many different beliefs about what is real and what is fantasy. Those who look at the world through the lens of a biblical worldview see actual reality. Those who see it through the lens of a different belief system see a mirage that to them appears real but is actually a fantasy. God has given believers the task of speaking into the many truth mirages in order that His will can be done on earth as it is in heaven.

Discussion Questions

1. What is the essential knowledge base Christians must possess to fulfill God's purpose in life?
2. What kinds of skills are necessary for Christians to develop in order to fulfill God's purpose for our lives?
3. How can people go about developing an individual plan for accomplishing the will of God in their life?
4. What must a person ultimately be willing to do in order to accomplish God's purpose?

Meet the Author

Freddy Davis is the president of MarketFaith Ministries. He is the author of numerous books and has a background as an international missionary, pastor, radio host, worldview trainer, and entrepreneur. Freddy is a graduate of Florida State University with a BS in Communication, and holds both Masters of Divinity and Doctor of Ministry degrees from Southwestern Baptist Theological Seminary. He is a popular speaker, particularly on the topic of worldview and its practical implications for the Christian life. He lives in Tallahassee, FL with his wife Deborah.

CPSIA information can be obtained
at www.ICGtesting.com
Printed in the USA
BVHW041643280322
632432BV00004B/5/J